Lionel Abrahams, who was born in Johannesburg
in 1926, has made rich contributions to South
African letters. As the founder of a literary
magazine and two small presses, he is considered
to have begun a new era of recognition of
poetry by black writers — Oswald Mtshali and
Mongane Wally Serote, among others.
He is himself a noted poet, having produced
three volumes: *Thresholds of Tolerance* (1975),
Journal of a New Man (1984) and *The Writer in
Sand* (1988). With Nadine Gordimer, he
co-edited *South African Writing Today* for Penguin
Books.

The Celibacy
of Felix Greenspan

The Celibacy
of Felix Greenspan

A Novel in Seventeen Stories

by Lionel Abrahams

Academy Chicago Publishers

Published in 1993 by
Academy Chicago Publishers
363 West Erie Street
Chicago, Illinois 60610

Library of Congress Cataloguing in Publication Data:
Abrahams, Lionel.
    The celibacy of Felix Greenspan / by Lionel
Abrahams.
        p.   cm.
    Originally published: Johannesburg: Bateleur Press,
        1977.
    ISBN 0-89733-396-9 : $21.95
    1. Physically handicapped—South Africa—Fiction.
        2. Jewish men—South Africa—Fiction.   I. Title.
PR9369.3.A18C45   1993
823—dc20   93-31454
                                            CIP

The Celibacy
of Felix Greenspan

Contents

The Other Windows

In the old house once, Moh had walked him to a corner of the garden where there was a little rockery in a loop of the pathway. It was a journey to America, she had told him. "Let's go to America and see all the wonders."

She had walked him around the rockery twice, then stood him between the stones on the lowest of the three dry beds.

And that was a journey.

America?

America?

The three rings of stones were mysterious: on one stone a paint-smear of dried moss, the withered trumpet of an iris leaf dangling through a gap from the top bed to the one below, and, amid the paperiness, the vibrating flamepoint of an untwisting purple bud. The house, from this new angle, the verandah and the windows, looked different, and the garden so big and strange . . .

It was hardly twenty steps to America.

But approaching the Children's Hospital, seeing the red brick building loom and stretch behind the wrought-iron top of the long street wall,

entering the tall gates, he was dizzy and frightened as if he were the pink child on a navy blue
moulded plaque high on one blank façade, and
hung over an empty silence nearly as deep as the
one where the sky was that cold colour. The car,
as it came through the gates, commanded im-
portantly, "Husssh . . .!" anxiously continuing the
sound while it crossed the gravelled area and
pushed into a parking space. The garden — lawn,
palm and path — to be glimpsed down one side
beyond a corner of the building, was empty,
square and still. The hospital's rows of sliding
windows were like solemn eyes half-closed while
the least possible noise was being made.

A part of the building had a steep tiled roof. They
crossed its polished black stoep, and glass swing-
doors let them into the hospital smell, into the
bareness of hushed waiting-rooms whose white
walls turned all the brisk and timid murmurings
to echoes, and pale-grey corridors leaping with
a squeal of rubber, radiator by radiator, into
the gloom, into the depths of the building.

Somewhere in the chill he felt kisses. Somewhere
through the hum and rustle of the uniformed
people's quiet hurrying he called out, and everything that Moh and Daddy said became knotted
into, "Soon, darling! Soon . . ."

Soon?

It was a sound that came of itself, echoing off
the smooth, high walls . . . and they were gone.

He was on a rubber-wheeled trolley passing a-
long a corridor with glimpses of white rooms. He
saw as he passed another waiting trolley with a

boy lying on it, and someone in white was stroking his hair. "Well, Joseph Anthony, are you back again?" she said with terrible kindness.

At last there was a bed. He snatched at sleep.

How long was he in that little room? Two days? Twice they came with the smell of methylated spirits and a steady purple flame and a needle which drew a drop of stinging blood from his thumb.

Then he was in a vast room with rows of beds.

He lay and listened to other children talking about things he did not know yet: Dinkey Toys and Meccano sets and operations and visiting. He saw them looking at comics and throwing things from bed to bed, and opening strange round boxes out of which poured heaps of smooth sticks and wooden rounds that they built into windmills. Across such spaces would he dare to call back to them? He did, a little, reaching out from the wide silence of watching and waiting on what was happening to him.

He felt even through his sleep the stiffness of his bed and starchy sheets. And he wakened to the lights breaking into the last of the night with the first wash, with the splashing, the protesting and crying of the children, the strong impatient movements of the nurses and their low-voiced conversation with each other across their work.

That was every day. And so was the unacceptable taste of the meals that came in deep bowls, and the comedy when the canvas-clothed Zulus came to move all the beds out of place and thumpingly polish the floor.

But there were also the things that happened only once. A day when a man came into the ward with a bunch of whispering bright balloons and there was one for him, yellow, and real under his hand and threatening. And once he was awake when it was dark, late, later even than eight o' clock. There was a sound of snoring far across the ward. And from away, away in the midst of the stillness came the thin crying of a baby.

And then, coming through the door into the ward slowly like two more strangers but bursting toward him when they saw where he was, Moh and Daddy with him again for the first visiting time — just a few minutes that seemed far, far off as soon as they were over. He had something sweet to eat. He swam in the music of Moh's voice reading the Sunday comics to him. Mavis's and Becky's names, when Daddy spoke about them, sounded like people he had never seen. He lay sticky and trembling afterwards, until the nurses came, brisk with thermometers and basins, and tumbled him to smooth his bed. Another visiting time Moh and Daddy told him about a lorry. It had run up the pavement and bumped their fence and their wall. How did that look? he wondered, how did *that* look? The fence was broken. That was terrible, fearful! They left him a book that had a black cat on the cover. No, the soft flat book was shaped like a cat, it *was* a black cat, cut out. When it opened there were two black cats. All the pages inside were white cats.

But more mysterious, what he longed most of

all to know about were the other windows.

One morning he sat in his bed and looked through a window in front of him into the dewy first of the daylight. Perhaps a screen had been moved away, or a blind was lifted, or it was when the Zulus moved his bed. Suddenly, across a straight cool garden with beds of cannas, he saw part of a red-brick building facing him, and in it was a row of windows. They were windows with white, perfect frames and plain white curtains looped up around the dimness beyond.

Perhaps he saw them yet another time, or even twice more, and perhaps figures behind them. Once, while he stared, one of the children in the ward stretched up to a window sill and shouted loudly across the garden, and in one of those windows something white flickered and a tiny joyous voice called back. Who were the happy people there, what kind of place could it be that they were in, in the shadowiness behind those windows? If he waited and watched closely enough and long enough, perhaps he would find out.

But the day came when he was taken up from his bed and dressed in his clothes to go home at last. Going home was so exciting that he wanted, whenever he had to speak, to shout instead and laugh at something. He was wheeled along unrecognisable passages and into a lift; the door closed, and when it opened there was a different place outside, a strange green vestibule decorated with photographs, where Daddy was waiting. Yet they came out at the same glassed swing doors

on the tile-roofed porch of the hospital. Beyond
the polished black stoep was the gravel and Daddy's motor car with Mavis inside standing behind
Daddy's seat, very shy.

Reaching home, the new house in the new half-
built street, he saw the deep tracks of the wheels
in the damp earth of the pavement, and the
bent fence still sagging against the verandah wall.
That was what the lorry had done. There. There!
And he saw the veld behind the houses, fresh
green on the overcast day, and the grass on the
pavement, flat like ragged rugs but heaping up
high along the fence. Somewhere, perhaps in
that grass, there were crickets chirping, and from
down in the veld came the clank and creak of the
windmill.

Inside the house everything was so small! And
there were kittens. He peered through the gloom
to see the new kittens, weird, weird, in the laun-
dry-basket behind the bathroom door. And the
rooms were all tiny. How did they all get into
this kitchen? Moh and Daddy and Mavis and the
baby and he and the table and chairs and the
stove and the sink? And there was the light
hanging down!

But at night in bed waiting for sleep, he was
filled again with the mystery of those windows at
the hospital — with all the mysteries of the whole
hospital which flooded into his feelings like
smells of polish and spirits and disinfectants, but
most of all with the mystery of the windows a-
cross the garden that were as remote as the pattern of white canals on a planet.

Adventure One

One afternoon when Moh had put Felix down
in the yard, leaving him the broken knife and the
big spoon to dig a hole with, he thought of something. He remembered Uncle Harry (who was
magic because he could make things disappear
or pull pennies out of your ear or anywhere) telling them that if you put petrol in a hole it could
make little tunnels under the ground.

He shouted, "Mommy, come and pick me up.
I've got a good idea."

"Oh, you nuisance," Moh said, coming to the
kitchen door after he had called her twice more.
"What do you want?"

"I want," he said, "to go to Uncle Harry's shop
by myself with Letty and get a bottle of petrol."

"Did you ever hear!" Moh said. "That's an impossible idea. Just forget about it."

"Why?" he wailed. "It's *not* impossible." He knew
that when they drove there (which was often, because Daddy did some business about some new
houses in Westdene) once they got to the Brixton
main road the car went straight all the way till
they saw, by itself on an island in the traffic, the
pointy red building with the petrol pumps out-

side. The more Moh said no the more he argued and cried, until she slapped her forehead and said, "Oy, you make me sick and tired. Now look, petrol is not for playing with and garages don't give it away. Put this silly idea out of your head."

"I want to buy it I mean," Felix explained. "I'm not going to play with it. I *need* it . . . for something. Call Letty to take me."

"Letty won't take you. She's got her own things to do now."

"She will. She takes me with her when she goes to Vrededorp."

"She doesn't know the way to Uncle Harry's shop."

"But I know it," Felix shouted.   "When you get up there to the gravy-yard it's just straight.   I *know* the way."

"Obstinate child, it's further than Vrededorp. It's too far for Letty to walk. You'll never get there. Now don't be silly."

"We will get there. It's near. I *want* to go. LETTY! Call her. Give me a tickey. LETTY COME AND PUSH ME IN THE PRAM!"

Even after Letty and Moh had stopped teasing him and laughing at him to make him change his mind, and Letty had said, "Orright, I'll take you — don't cry," and got herself ready and put him in the pram, Moh still said, as she put a tickey in the pocket of his overalls, "Waste of money! Anyway, they won't sell you a little bottle of petrol."

"They will, they will," Felix shouted. "It's my own uncle's shop."

"Oh, well," Moh said, "You're so obstinate. Find

out for yourself." And Letty laughed and they were off.

First they went up to the cemetery, which was also the way to Vrededorp, and then they turned left into the big road. This way they passed along more of the graveyard fence. Under tall black moaning trees the gravestones and mounds lay in shade and sunshine. When Felix shot past in Daddy's car he never saw how full of secrets and terrible the baking red mounds were. He didn't like to look at them.

Past that fence the road went into Brixton between houses and empty patches. It looked wider than on other days and when a bus or lorry passed it looked bigger.

"You see, Letty," Felix shouted, "I told you this is the way."

"This is the right way, hey," Letty said, nodding.

"Yes! Gee . . ." And Felix sang, "I'm going to Uncle Harry's shop, I'm going to Uncle Harry's shop. Will he be *surprised*!"

It was the right road but in the car it was covered so quickly. Now it spread and stretched. Here they were four blocks along from the cemetery and he knew they were still near the beginning. It was the right road, the one he knew that ran with little bends but never a corner all the way to the island with the shop full of furniture and the petrol pumps. But if it looked so much wider and longer today, then would it still lead to the same place? Wouldn't this be like getting into a lift and finding the world changed when the door opened?

When they came to the sixth block Letty asked, "It's this way? You sure?"

Felix answered, "Yes, yes! I *know* the way!"

After nine blocks she said, "Aren't you lost?"

"No!" Felix screamed. "I'm not lost! This is the way Daddy always, always drives! *You* don't know, Letty!"

Letty pushed on and the road kept on stretching and stretching. He had seen every bit of it before but never before had all the places he recognized been so far apart. Suddenly Letty said, "It's too far."

"No, no, it's not far," Felix wailed. "It's up here. Turn this way."

"Up here?" said Letty, and turned off from the main road. After two blocks she asked, "Now where?" and Felix told her to turn again, and then he made her turn at every corner they came to. For a long time they zigzagged deeper and deeper into a strange suburb. Felix was frightened, but he went on and on doing it long after he knew he could never find his way back. He didn't notice how the sun was sinking until Letty said, "We can't get petrol now, it's getting dark. Let's go home."

Felix giggled. "But we're lost," he said.

Letty gave a short laugh. "*You're* lost," she said as she turned the pram around. The journey home was much straighter and shorter than Felix expected. They stopped twice on the way. Once so that Felix could spend his tickey at a sweet shop. And once alongside the cemetery fence for Letty to fasten up his shirt because it was growing cold.   It was now too dark to see the mounds, but he said, "Don't stop here.   It's the gravy-yard."

Letty laughed. "Are you frightened?" But she did his shirt and then she pushed on, laughing again and again.

A Big Boy Now

"My mother never fastens the top button of my shirt at home," said Felix.

And the nurse who was dressing him — in clothes that were not his own: plain khaki clothes — replied, "Well, you're not at home now," and fastened the uncomfortable button just the same.

At first, after arriving at the big stone building that was like a castle, he had been put among the babies. There were only eight of them. They were taken up from their part of the grounds by the nurses at half past three to be bathed, and ate supper in their pyjamas on high chairs. They had to go to bed early and were not allowed to play with the bigger children. And they were taken at a separate time — the three who could not walk piled into one big black pram — for their walk on the private road along the little, chalky cliff cut into the pine-wooded slope of the koppie.

At home Felix had warned Moh: "Tell them they mustn't press hard when they brush my hair," and another time: "Tell them they must only give me *weak* tea." But he *had* begun to drink tea already, like Daddy, instead of just milk, and sitting in the playground dust, after his ginger snap or marie biscuit was eaten up, he felt it wasn't fair that he should be separated with the babies.

But one day the Native boys brought two blackboards and easels and a lot of little tables and chairs from the storeroom and put them in the two huge playrooms, and then school began again after the holidays. Felix was old enough to start going to school, so he could not be among the babies any longer. He was given a bed downstairs in the dormitory for the smallest boys.

Johnny, one of the biggest boys, who was fourteen, looked after him and carried him on his back to the bottom or top lawn, to the dining room, to the lavatories and to school. There was also a big girl named Pikkie who would kiss Felix's cheeks and tell everyone he was her little sweetheart. He sat by her whenever he could. Because really he was too small to play with the others. Anyone could beat him in a wrestle, and even in a race across the lawn against others who also only crawled, he never won.

Once, though, he knew, just for a moment, what it felt like to be the winner in something. It was a day near the end of the school term. The two teachers took all the children down to bottom lawn, and there, on the edge of the gardens that overlooked the valley, they had all sorts of races and competitions, and besides everyone being given a packet of sweets, the winners got prizes. There were games for everybody and at last Felix was put onto a chair in front of a blackboard which had a pig drawn on it. A yellow duster was tied around his eyes and he was given a piece of chalk. He had to make a cross where the pig's eye should be. When the duster was taken off he thought that he had put his cross in the wrong place. But a teacher said, "That's very well done, Felix! You've got it just right." He had won. There was a blue clockwork racing car for a prize.

But someone said, "I'm sure he could peep."

"Could you see it, Felix?" the teacher asked.

"No," he replied, "I could just see the bottom of the board."

So he and another boy were blindfolded again. They made their crosses and then the blue racing car was given to the other boy.

But even if he did not win, he liked to join in everything he could. And he could join in the singing at school and on Sunday mornings, when a minister or a member of the committee came to preach and they had a service. One Sunday afternoon at visiting time he said to Moh and Daddy, "I can sing two songs," and he sang to them, first:

> Two lovely black eyes
> O, what a surprise!
> Only for telling a bundle of lies,
> Two lovely black eyes!

and then:

> Onward Christian soldiers
> Marching as to war
> With the cross of Jesus
> Going on before.

They told him that was a Christian hymn and he should not sing it. After that whenever they sang *Onward Christian Soldiers* at service, Felix stayed silent. But he joined in all the other songs.

Once when a group of children was about to be photographed for a picture in the Annual Report, he scurried across the lawn to sit next to Pikkie who made a place for him. Someone said, "Felix's not supposed to be in it," but he stayed and when he saw the picture in the Annual Report, he was glad Pikkie had made room for him, even though he had nearly spoiled the picture because he wanted to wee and moved just as the photo was taken and his knee was blurred. He could show everybody the picture with him in the front row.

He could be in the reading at school. He learnt his reading quickly and easily, and soon whenever any of the other children got stuck — even the boy who was ten years old and still in Grade One — the teacher would say, "Tell him, Felix," and he would read out the word.

At night in the little dormitory where eight of the smallest boys slept, he could join in the prayers. Night by night the little boys took turns in praying aloud for the whole dormitory before they went to sleep, Felix could take his turn too, and say a prayer like those he had heard the minister saying at the Sunday morning services. One night, even, after one of the other boys had said the prayer and everyone's hands were parted and eyes were open again, Felix said, "You can't pray properly. Why do you just ask God for everything? Why don't you say thank you for something?"

The other boy was shocked. "For what?" he demanded.

"For food and the sun and the birds and the flowers and everything."

"Ag, anybody can pray the way he wants to," said the biggest boy in the room.

"Yes," said the boy who had offered the prayer, "I never told you what to say."

"But I always say thank you for everything," said Felix.

"Ag, you!" the biggest boy burst out, "Your mother eats snakes!"

"She doesn't!" Felix gasped.

Another boy laughed. "She does. I saw her. Your mother eats snakes!"

The others joined in: "Your mother eats snakes!"

"Felix's mother eats snakes!"

It was a Saturday morning but it was raining, so instead of going to the lawns and up the koppie to play, the children went into the two playrooms where the tables and chairs for school were stacked up against the long walls. Because the bare windows gave a wide view of the sky, the playrooms were gloomy whenever the weather was gloomy; but big boxes of fancy-dress costumes and toys were brought in for the children to play with. There was a set of hundreds of little lead animals, with buildings and fences and trees and carts and farmers.

A lot of the boys began to lay out a big farm. There were so many pieces that Felix could help too. He had put four cows in a row next to a hedge, and he was going to crawl around another boy's part to fetch a milkmaid from the box, when his stomach began to hurt. He tried to call Johnny McKay to take him to the lavatory, but it was too late already; his stomach was loose.

He sat a while uneasily by his hedge and four cows. Then he said to a boy who was putting a plough and a tree on the other side of the cows, "Wait, I'm just going to do something," He crawled across to the corner next to the big fireplace above which hung a picture of Jesus with all the disciples, and with his face to the corner he prayed for the mess to vanish, for it not to have happened, or for it never to be found out . . .

He went back to his hedge and his cows. But there was a smell, and a damp trail marked the floor where he crawled. Very soon someone said, "Sis, Felix has messed his pants!"

"I haven't . . ." he muttered hopelessly.

But already there was a chorus: "Yes you have!"

"Sis! Look!"

"Isn't he a baby!"

And the nurse was coming from the other end of the playroom to see what was the matter.

He was carried away to the bathroom, cleaned, and then put to bed in the little dormitory for the rest of the day. He lay and listened to the wind moaning among the pine trees, and gazed at the ceiling making out faces of sailors and fat babies in the moulded design.

A nurse came into the dormitory with a pile of clean sheets and pillow-cases.

"Oh, Felix," she said when she saw him. "What's the matter, my boy, are you sick?"

"No."

"Then why are you in bed? Are you being punished?"

"Yes."

"But you're not a naughty boy. What did you do?"

Felix looked down and said nothing.

"Tell me what you did, Felix?"

"I — I hit another boy," said Felix, "smaller than me."

"Oh, is that what you did?" said the nurse. "You should be ashamed of yourself."

And Felix tried to look ashamed.

Some Milk Pudding

In the kitchen the children were eating their supper of omelettes, milk pudding and cocoa. Felix was still finishing off his omelette when he saw that Mavis and Becky were both drinking their cocoa already.

"Ag, Mommy," he said, "I don't want any milk pudding."

Because this annoyed Moh, he paused to empty his cup of cocoa before leaving the table. Then he stumped across to the kitchen window, pulled himself up and leaned gazing out in silence for a long time. A bare wire fence less than a yard away separated him from the pavement, so he could see the faces and hear the voices of all who passed. He saw working people coming home, lots of them with dark-coloured shirts and caps and sandwich tins and thermos flasks; and groups of noisy youths. Also there were some Natives sitting on the pavement and some others hurrying past. He wondered if they were walking all the way to Sophiatown.

At the same time he was watching how the light changed from thin yellow to purple velvet. He saw orange fire, from the setting sun, fill the dull window panes of the house across the street, then break up and fade away; and he saw how, like a sudden stab into the creeping darkness, the street lights came on.

Suddenly he said, "Here's Daddy!"

There was a shout from Mavis and Becky, and when Daddy entered the back door his hand was grabbed by one of them and his parcel by the other, before he had said hullo. He said it though, three times, "Hullo, hullo, hullo" and kissed them all and put down his newspaper and went to wash his hands at the sink and asked, "Well, what did you do today? Hey, Felix, what can you tell me?"

And so they told him.

Noel who lived a block away had come with his Doberman pinscher to play. They played in the backyard and the untarred side street with its grassy pavements. They had a rope which they tied to the fence for jumping games, and all the time they threw things for Noel's dog to run after and smell.

Then half-way through the afternoon, there came, "Heh, what you doing?" Sacred, the Venda piccanin, had finished washing dishes and was free now, until it was time to start cooking his own mealie meal, to spend a while with Felix. The others ran up and talked for a while, but soon went back to their games.

Sacred and Felix went to the back verandah steps and sat in the sun. Sacred brought out his pipe and filled it and lit it as they began to talk. While he smoked he kept blowing gingerly and scowling and spitting. Felix asked him, "Why do you do that?"

"The peep she is broken," Sacred answered, pointing to the snapped stem. "The smoke is too hot."

Felix nodded and they went on talking about Sacred's brother who worked in Germiston and the farm near Louis Trichardt that Sacred came from and Daddy's car and Uncle Lewis's sickness and the soapbox cart Felix was going to get and the kite he wanted to make. When Sacred rubbed his tongue on the back of his wrist and emptied the pipe out, Felix said, "Gee, I wish I could buy you a new one!"

He turned just then to look at Mavis and Noel. All the time they had been throwing bits of coal for the Doberman. Now, suddenly tired of that, the pair of them were climbing from the top of the coal heap onto the roof of the lavatory.

When Sacred saw them he said, "Heh, no Mehvees! Don't go up there."

Breathing hard, Mavis blurted. "Ag, man, I will." In a moment she reached the roof safely, so he just repeated, "Heh, no . . ." and left it at that.

Felix was asking him something. "Hey, and when they finished picking the fruit and stuff on the farm, what do they do with it? Do they put it on a wagon and bring it here to sell?"

"Uh! No," exclaimed Sacred with amusement. "Is too far here Johannesburg for the wagon."

Mavis and Noel had brought bits of coal up to the roof to throw to the dog. But he was not really interested. So very soon they stopped and whispered together for a while. Mavis giggled and suddenly threw down a piece of coal. It landed very close to Sacred.

He hunched his shoulders and, laughing, protested, "Uh! No!"

But Mavis threw more coal and Noel joined in until Sacred sprang up frightened, exclaiming, "Heh-heh! No!" Then a piece hit him and he said with puzzlement in his voice, "Ha, what is matter? You mad? Uh! Don't throw me!"

"Mavis, stop that!" Felix was screaming. "You, Noel! I'll break your neck!"

And Noel replied in a mocking tone, "Pteh, pteh, pteh, pteh!" showing his tongue.

Another few pieces of coal came down and suddenly Sacred stooped and picked up the broken rubber band of a pram wheel from the ground and struck two or three times over the edge of the low roof at Noel. Suddenly Noel gave a loud high scream and scrambled down from the roof. Sobbing and screaming and clutching his leg he ran out of the yard towards his own house, while his dog ran after him.

The back door opened and Moh came onto the little cement verandah. "What's the matter?" she asked.

Felix and Sacred told her while Mavis climbed down off the roof. When she knew what had happened she said to Mavis, "My golly, that's bad. You mustn't throw stones."

Mavis, hanging her head a little, said, "Noel's daddy's a policeman."

"He's not a policeman," Felix said. "He's a tram driver."

"Well, he can catch you," said Mavis.

"They're sure to make trouble," Moh said to

Sacred.

"Uh, is shame," he said, shaking his head. "They will catch me. I not stay here. No, goo'pye, Meesees Sees, No, goo'pye, Felix . . ." and he ran suddenly from the yard.

After a while Moh said, "I'm making a milk pudding for you for supper," and she bent down to pick up Sacred's pipe which he had left behind on the verandah step and went inside.

About half an hour later Noel returned with his father. He was in his shirt-sleeves and had an angry scowl on his face. "Where's your boy?" he asked.

"He's gone away," Mavis said. So he turned and went home again, while Noel stayed to play some more. Everybody felt like going to the veld and the tall bluegum trees behind the Native hospital, but Noel wanted them to go down to the ash veld and play kennetjie, and the argument went on and on until a tented wagon drawn by a team of donkeys came through the dip.

Up the road that meandered between the ash-covered refuse dump and the open veld behind the hospital, it came creaking and rumbling out of Mayfair West. There was a ragged little black touleier, and a dusty-looking white boy up in front holding a whip. And a man whose old hat half hid his eyes trudged alongside shouting repeatedly, "Pere . . . pere . . . Mooi perskes . . . twee sjielings 'n maandjie," in a distant-sounding voice.

You could see, too, what his peaches and pears were like by the one or two that were stuck onto a forked twig fixed upright on the front of the wagon. The children leaned over the wall of the verandah where they had gathered and called as the wagon passed:

"Hey, donkey, look at me!"

"Ah shame! They small, hey?"

"I wish I had one . . ."

"Perskies, pteh, pteh, pteh, pteh!" Noel shouted, suddenly pushing his stomach forward and marching up and down. It was very loud and mocking, and after a bit Felix said, "Ah, Noel, shut up!" But Noel's noise continued until the roar of a red and cream bus drowned the last creaks and cries from the disappearing wagon.

When he knew what had happened Daddy said angrily to Mavis, "It would serve you right if he hit you. You're a naughty girl! I'll give you a hiding the next time you throw stones!"

"It wasn't stones," said Mavis, again hanging her head a little, "it was only coal."

After that Moh took Mavis and Becky to their bath, and while Daddy ate his supper, Felix went once more to stand at the window.

Suddenly there came a knock at the back door, and when Daddy opened it, there was Sacred.

"Oh, Sacred, so you came back?"

"Yes, baas," replied Sacred, smiling shyly.

"So, you were frightened, hey? You ran away."

"No, my seh," Sacred protested. "I'm going see for my frien' here for West Street."

"Oh, I see . . . Now, I suppose you want to eat something?"

"Yes, please."

"Well, I'll go ask the missus," said Daddy, and he went round to the bathroom.

"Hullo," Felix said to Sacred.

"Yes, hullo, Felix," said Sacred.

"Oh, there's your pipe," said Felix, pointing to the top of the refrigerator.

"Thank you, my baas," Sacred said, taking the pipe. "Ha, I'm forget, heh?"

"Yes," said Felix.

Just then Moh entered the kitchen and said to Sacred, "Hullo. It's too late for you to make mealie meal now. You'd better have bread."

So Sacred took bread and meat and a mug of coffee, joked once or twice more with Daddy, said, no he did not need a candle, and carefully carrying the plate and the mug with two thick slices of bread balanced on top of it, went out to his room.

Suddenly, a little guiltily, Felix said to Moh as she came out of the pantry, "Ah, Moh, you know what I feel like now?"

"What?" Moh asked.

Throwing his head back a little he dragged his words, "I'd . . . like . . . some . . . pudding. Can I have some?"

Miracles

"Felix, you're going home," announced a nurse coming into the playroom with a wheel-chair.

"Yippee!" Felix yelled. Then he stared at her face and said, "Ah Nurse Stevens, you're bluffing. It's not even holidays or anything."

"Well, it's true. Come on, hop in. Don't argue."

While she was wheeling him, he asked, "How long am I going home for?"

"Forever."

In the car Daddy told him there was an Australian lady doctor who was going to cure him. He had to go to her three times a week for treatment and Matron wouldn't allow any child to go out three times a week to a doctor who wasn't one of The Home's doctors. That was why he had to leave forever.

The Australian doctor gave him rough massage and hard exercises and forced him to stand and try to walk no matter how scared he was. She was even stricter than Miss Duncan in the massage room at The Home.

Moh said, "You can be sure she knows what she's doing. Nothing comes easy. She'll get results."

But the lady doctor did not cure him, because she suddenly had to go back to Australia.

He was home for ever, and it was hard work for Moh. She knew how to walk him more comfortably than any of the nurses or big boys at The Home or Daddy. They held him up by gripping his arms just below the shoulders. She liked to slip her forearms under his armpits and clasp her hands over his chest. And she always walked at the right speed. But now that he was taller and heavier it tired her to walk him for too long. His head kept thumping her chest, especially if he talked.

So they got Sacred to help him dress and go to the lav and the places where he wanted to play. If it was to the park Sacred would drag or push him in his soapbox cart. If it was only down into the veld, to the sloots or the koppie or the windmill or the bluegums and peppercorn near the Native hospital, he would walk him.

The school Mavis went to wouldn't take him so he had to have a teacher at home. Miss Ordman came twice a week and gave him Standard 1 lessons and homework and taught him to write with a giant pencil on paper instead of chalk on a slate.

Moh and Daddy kept looking for someone to cure him. They read in a newspaper about a German doctor called a quack that hundreds of people were going to. Four times, leaving early in the cold dark mornings, Daddy and Felix drove to his house in Krugersdorp. But each time he only sold them little pills and a big bottle of cod liver oil for lots of money and told them to come back again.

Nearly every evening on his way home from his shop in Newlands Uncle Harry dropped in to visit them for a little while. He was always full of tricks and jokes and stories and surprises, except when he and Moh were talking about the rest of the family or Russia. Some of his tricks were just clever, like when he balanced a cigarette on his forehead and let it fall, the right way for smoking, into his mouth. One that frightened Felix was when he poured some petrol on the bare ground in the yard and threw down a lighted match and then danced about among the tall roaring flames, without burning his trousers or his shoes one bit. But some of his tricks were real magic, like the time when he began by pulling a penny out of Becky's ear, which was an old trick, and then pulled another coin out of the penny and then a charm out of the other coin and on and on until there was a whole pile of treasure on the kitchen table.

His most magic trick of all was done one of the evenings when Daddy was not yet home from business. Uncle Harry placed a doorstop in the middle of the empty passage, then he and Moh held a sheet stretched across the passage. He sang some magic words in a loud voice and then dropped the sheet, and there, on the spot marked by the doorstop, was Daddy.

The children screamed, and when Felix got his breath back he said, "But HOW?"

Grinning and winking, Uncle Harry said, "Magic."

"But, Daddy," Felix said, "How did you come?"

"I came up through the floor."

"Gee, Uncle Harry," Felix said, "I didn't know you could do real magic, with people."

"Oh, you donkey," Moh said. "I'm surprised at you."

"Why?" said Felix. "Why? It's real magic . . ."

One day Daddy and Moh took Felix to be examined by a clever specialist in Pasteur Chambers. When they came away Moh was crying. At home she lay on the sofa and cried all day, even more than when Auntie Jessica died. Once she squeezed him very tight and said, "Oh Felix! What you could be if you were normal." But mostly she didn't look at him, and did nothing for him and Mavis and Becky. He felt frightened and very cross with the specialist.

The tall black piano at Auntie Thelma's house was really Moh's. Auntie Thelma had it because she was lonely and because Moh had no room for it when she was first married. When Auntie Thelma got a new piano, the old one, with its two sculpture faces of men with long hair stuck on the front, came back to Moh. The other furniture in the dining room was squashed up and the piano just managed to fit in a corner. The little seat that came with it was full of old paper music. Moh carefully smoothed out some crumpled sheets and stuck them together where they were torn. And sometimes when she was tired, instead of going for a nap, she practiced her old pieces: A Maiden's Prayer, The Witch's Flight, Pale Hands I

Love, I Dre-heamt I Dwe-helt in Mar-harble Halls,
Cavalliera Rusticana . . . Cavalliera Rusticana was
the most beautiful and The Witch's Flight was
the most exciting, when Moh's fingers raced and
the music swooped and swooped from the dining-
room out to the street, up to the tall trees at the
Native hospital that Felix could see from the window, and even as far as the pines and cypresses
at the cemetery.

They were picnicking beside one of the little
lakes at Heidelberg Kloofs. Moh was in the water
with Felix and Becky watching them while they
splashed around. When Felix kneeled up the
water came to his navel and when he kneeled
down it came to his chest. Becky wanted to go out
and Moh took her. Felix, kneeling up, was stump-
ing a few steps along when he overbalanced and
the water swallowed him. Moh and Daddy (in his
clothes) came after him. They got in each other's
way and screamed and scratched each other, but
at last they had him out.

When they could talk Moh said, "I was trying
to dive under him and lift him on my back. Why
did you pull me away?"

And Daddy said, "I thought you were drowning
too. Why did you scratch me like that?"

"Oh, you fool!" Moh said. "You could have
drowned us all."

Lying on the grass, wrapped in towels, with arms
hugging him and hands stroking him, Felix was
still being swallowed and swept away and suffocated by the water. No matter what was done for
him, this went on happening inside him. As they

drove away he saw the sun low behind trees. It
was an empty orange balloon. And everything
else, even the car, even the ground, even Daddy
and Moh, was an empty balloon.

Moh said, "It's a miracle you didn't drown us
all."

A neighbour told them about the faith healer. He
was an old farmer who lived near Brits. Felix was
very interested to meet a real farmer. He supposed
he would be like the one in Tiger Tim's Annual,
with a beard and a floppy hat and over-alls and a
pitchfork. He asked Moh and Daddy a lot of
questions about farmers.

"Don't you want to know about faith healers?"
Moh asked.

"I know," said Felix, who had heard the neighbour explain.

On a Sunday afternoon the whole family, with the
neighbour to show them the way, drove to the
faith healer's farm. There was even a real pig-sty
with stinky pigs and a lot of mud just a little way
from the farmhouse. Felix was a little surprised
that the farmer wasn't working outside. He wasn't
even waiting in the doorway to welcome them. An
old lady in a black dress let them into a room
where some other people were sitting on chairs
along the walls.

They waited a long time. More people came in
and sat down. Every now and again an inside
door opened and a tall old man peeped out and
called one of the waiting people to him.

At last he pointed to Felix. Daddy walked him to

the door where the old man took him by the arm. He sent Daddy back to his seat and closed the door and they were in a small room with a bed. The old man took off Felix's trousers and put him face down on the bed.

"Now, little boy," he said, "pray."

Felix could not put his hands together but he closed his eyes and whispered, "Please, God . . . Please, God . . ."

The faith healer began praying in Afrikaans and his huge hands with vaseline on them came down on Felix and massaged his back and bottom and legs as though they were squeezing a big lump of plasticene into a new shape. Waves of tingling shot through Felix to his bones and along his skin. The hands gave a last strong squeeze and were suddenly lifted.

"Stand!" the faith healer commanded.

Felix had never stood without help, but now he rose from the bed by himself and stood up.

"Walk!" the faith healer commanded.

Felix took not just three or four shaky steps but pace after pace in a real walk.

"Dank die Here," said the faith healer, and opened the door into the waiting room. Felix, still without his trousers, walked into the room. "Vriende," the faith healer said, "dank die Here!" And everybody began to talk at once and shake hands with the faith healer and Daddy and Moh, whose eyes kept getting full of tears even though she was smiling.

For the rest of that day they visited uncles and aunts and Felix walked across rooms and down passages and along verandahs and everybody kept saying, "Wonderful!" "Isn't it wonderful?" The next day at home without the excitement it was still real: he was nervous, but whenever he felt brave enough he stood up and walked from room to room. On the third day and for a few days after that he could still practice walking along a safe narrow strip between the sofa and the wall. But when he wanted to go anywhere he stumped on his knees or called Sacred just as always.

One day when Miss Ordman was expected, Felix called Sacred to walk him out to the secret rock chair he had discovered on the little koppie beyond the veld. There he sat hiding because he hadn't done any of his homework. It was the first time he had done none at all, though Miss Ordman had been disappointed with him before for not doing everything she'd asked of him, because with only two lessons a week he couldn't get on unless he did homework.

He came down when he saw Moh and Miss Ordman come out on the veld and heard Moh shout for him. Moh's tight lips showed how angry she was. "Oh, shocking! Shocking behaviour!" she said. "Hiding away. Wasting Miss Ordman's time. It's disrespectful, do you realize? I thought you had more responsibility. I didn't expect you to run away from a little homework . . . .What's going to become of him if he can't do the things he has to?"

She and Miss Ordman talked about it for a long time and then the teacher wrote out a timetable to help him do a little homework every day. He promised to follow it, but after a few days Moh had to say, "Come on, homework time — why do I have to nag you?" before he would begin.

When Miss Ordman stopped coming, there was Mr Keyser from Mavis and Becky's school and after him Mr Biljon who was very strict and not interesting.

One day Felix said, "I think I'd better go back to The Home so that I can go to school."

"Oh, what a sensible boy!" Moh said. He had been home a year and a half.

On his first holiday he said he had changed his mind and begged to be allowed to stay home and promised to work hard. But Moh said, "You missed your chance. In any case, I'm worn out — I need a rest from you."

The day he was to go back he stumped away to the next corner and hid behind a little hedge. When Daddy came to that very corner and stood just a few feet away, looking up and down both streets with a puzzled look on his face, Felix couldn't help giggling, and that is how he was found.

He struggled and screamed all the way to The Home, and once there he did nothing for four days but cry and moan, "I want to go home . . . I want to go home! . . ." But it was too late.

When he saw that nothing could save him from being back, Felix set about doing his best at school and in the massage room. Something he couldn't understand was Miss Duncan, the head of the mas-sage room, always saying that he improved beauti-fully during term time but slipped back and lost it all whenever he went home on holiday. Anyway, he was improving. At massage he stood for longer and longer without falling, and sometimes he took six whole steps.

One rainy afternoon when the children were in the big playroom he stood up from his chair sud-denly and was walking. Matron came later and shook him by the hand in a joking way and said, "Mazeltov, Mr Greenspan," and when Miss Dun-can saw him next morning she said, "Bravo, Felix!" But leaving the dining-room after lunch he tripped, fell flat and bloodied his nose, and was left afraid to stand.

He had been back a whole year when, on a Sun-day during visiting, Moh told him she had had a dream about him walking. Two mornings later, having dressed himself, he was waiting beside his bed for Ashley, the boy who always walked him through to breakfast. Ashley seemed late, and Felix thought, "Why should I wait?" He stood up and walked through the dormitories, along one corridor, past the entrance hall, along another corridor, across the lawn, through the big play-room and into the dining room, just in time for grace.

On the Sunday after the next, which was visit-ing again, Felix surprised Moh and Daddy by walking to meet them. He and Moh said together, "The dream came true."

That year's Annual Report had two pictures of Felix. In one he was on his knees: "As he came to us — crawling." In the other he was standing: "NOW!"

Now it was for ever.

The next time he was home on holiday, he was walking along the pavement with Moh when a passing Native girl said, "Auw, shame!"

"What's she saying shame for?" asked Felix. "I can walk."

"Yes, you can walk," said Moh. "But don't you realize, you're still not normal?"

The Messiah

On Sunday mornings and Wednesday evenings there was Service, run by a member of the committee or a real priest, in the big playroom. Being Jewish did not stop Felix from attending. He learnt that only faith was needed to save one's soul — faith in Jesus, who was so good and had such powers, and who was a Jew on top of everything else. The parts about him suffering and being crucified — by Jews — made Felix less comfortable. He wished those parts could be left out. Then service would be just as interesting and enjoyable to go to.

But those parts wouldn't be left out. They came into things every day, in a way, even when it wasn't prayers at school or grace at table or anything that was supposed to do with God. He was 'Jew-boy' and had to hear about Jews having long noses and being stingy and cheats, all because Jesus got crucified by those old Jews — even though it was the Romans who really did it.

The old carpenter boy, Moses, who had a wonderful workshop opposite the kitchens near the end of the drive, where he would do anything from fixing a crutch or the wheel of a wheelchair to sharpening a pencil, old Moses who walked with a limp because one of his thick muscley legs was shorter than the other, who was so clever with his hands and so kind that everybody loved him and he seemed like someone out of the Bible even though he was black — he said one day, while Felix could hear him, "No, I don't like Jews. They killed Jesus." The boys were always saying that and Felix felt half cross and half ashamed. But when Moses said it, it was much worse: it seemed to be true, and Christians and Jews had to hate each other.

All the same, Felix went on going to Service. He learned there about the lamb that had been lost being more precious to the shepherd than the ninety-nine that were never lost, and he heard about converted Jews. He decided to be a converted Jew and to believe in Jesus and love him. He said prayers in bed every night, and he knew that good Christians, apart from forgiving everyone who hurt them, had to try to save other souls by converting them too. So when he was home on holiday, one night he told Moh the parable about the one lost lamb and begged her to be converted also. She seemed uncomfortable about what he was saying, but she only laughed a little and went on not even believing in God. All the same, Felix hoped that he would be able to convert her one day. He knew that Daddy did believe in God because he sometimes said Jewish prayers; he did not try to convert him.

Once Felix heard something wonderful. It was

about the Messiah. The Jews believed that one day the Messiah would come to the world from heaven to save everyone. The Christians believed that the Messiah had already come and was Jesus. But they also believed that one day, any day, He would come again. When that happened, surely Christians and Jews would all believe the same thing and wouldn't need to hate each other any more.

The Messiah, when He came, must be Jewish, a Jewish Christian. So any Jewish boy, any day now, could be Him. Felix, loving Jesus and believing in Him with all his heart, as the ministers always begged everyone to (Felix's favourite was the committee member, Mr Cooper, who told wonderful stories and made him feel it would be lovely to go to exciting places with him) — believing so much in Jesus and always managing not to do anything naughty, and caring so much about Moses and the other Christians hating Jews, began to think that it might, it could, it must be him. The Messiah. Although nobody knew it yet, and he wasn't ready to tell anyone — he would know when it would be the right time to let the secret out — he, Fellx, was that special Jewish boy who was Jesus back in the world for the second time to make the different people love each other, and to cure all the cripples and blind people and do all sorts of miracles that would make everybody believe in God.

He loved it on Sundays and Wednesdays when the ministers told about the miracles Jesus had done and the stories He had told, or about people who had got converted in wonderful ways or been

helped by God when they were in trouble or had
been very brave about doing what they knew God
wanted them to do or about going on having faith
when something was making it very hard.   He
wished he had a chance to show his faith like those
strong believers, and he longed for the time when
he would be able to do miracles that would be
better than any of the tricks that he had seen
magicians do at concerts and parties. Waiting for
the day when he would show everyone that he was
the Messiah, he didn't mind so much any more
what the other boys said about Jews, or when they
said things like "Don't try to Jew me" when someone wanted to make a bargain that wasn't fair. They
were only the chaps at The Home, and they didn't
know his secret yet.   Anyway, one of the things
Christians had to do was to forgive those who
trespassed against them, so it proved that he had
faith because he was always forgiving the other
boys for all their insults.

Mr Fergusson was the chairman of the committee
and he came up to The Home much more often
than any of the other members. Sometimes he
came to show special visitors around, and sometimes to inspect with Matron if anything had to be
done to the building. Once or twice when some of
the biggest boys had done something extra bad, Mr
Fergusson came and shouted at them in his big
voice in a terribly angry way. He also came very
often to be the minister at Sunday morning
service.

He was a big, oldish man with grey hair who spoke
and sang in a strong Scotch accent. He always

seemed to wear the same greyish brown suit and, just like Moses, the old carpenter, he walked quickly but with a deep limp. He did not make his preaching as friendly and interesting as Mr Cooper, who came quite seldom and always looked as if everything he wore was brand new. But Felix could tell by the loudness of his voice when he preached and sang hymns and prayed, that he had very strong faith.

Felix also sang the hymns and choruses ("Build on the Rock" was the one he liked best, because of the bang they had to make for "earthquake SHOCK") as loudly as he could, so Mr Fergusson knew that he was there at service. He also knew — because Felix had been at The Home for years already — that he was Jewish: there were hardly ever any other Jewish children.

One Sunday morning Mr Fergusson preached the Bible story of Joseph and his brothers. He was at the part where the jealous elder brothers had put Joseph into the pit and were getting ready to kill him when the traders from Egypt came by. "When the eldest brother, Reuben, saw the traders," said Mr Fergusson, "he said to the others, Why should we kill Joseph, when we can sell him as a slave to these traders? Well, Jews, you know, they are ready to sell anything, even their brother — so they agreed to do as Reuben said. . ."

Felix gave a little jump. The boy on the bench next to him nudged him and he saw two other boys turn to look at him with quick grins on their faces. He heard nothing more of the preaching or prayers and did not join in the singing of the last hymn.

On Wednesdays service was after supper, so all the children had to go because there was nowhere else to be. It was always the same minister, Mr Harty, who was not a committee member but a real priest who wore a black shirt with a stiff white ring collar that none of the children could guess how he put on or took off. Mr Harty was telling them a long story in a serial, about the adventures of a man named Christian and his friend Faithful. Even after what had happened that Sunday morning, Felix didn't have to miss the rest of the story.

But on the next Sunday morning at service time, instead of being in the big playroom with all the others, Felix was sitting outside on the lawn looking at *Pip, Squeak and Wilfred's Annual*, and hearing the hymns and the preaching without being able to make out the words. It was Mr Cooper today, but that didn't matter.

No one else was outside until Nurse Verster came past on her way to the dormitories. When she saw him she said, "Hullo, Felix. Why aren't you at service?"

Felix tried to look up at her, but the sun shone into his eyes. "Because I'm Jewish," he said.

The Girls and the Boys

For Service on Sundays and Wednesdays and concerts or anything special in the big playroom the bed patients who weren't serious cases were brought to join in. The strong cleaning boys, two by two, carried the beds from the wards along the corridors and stood them in a white row along the back of the playroom. There were always some of the big girls from the Daphne Ward.

The other children sat in rows on the long scrubbed benches that were dragged in from the dining room plus the four that usually stood against the walls in the playroom. Often the beds were in place and the children were waiting on the benches for quite a long time before the minister came and the service began.

It was one of these times that two of the Daphne Ward girls began to tease Felix. He was looking round at them when one of them smiled at him, winked, and said, "Do you love me, Felix?"

He blushed and shook his head hard, but before he could turn away, the second one was also asking, "Don't you love me?" and winking and smiling.

"I'm sure you do . . . I'm sure you love me," the

first girl was going on.

Felix turned away, waving his hands around his ears like chasing flies to make them stop, and thank goodness the minister came in just then and they had to leave him alone. When Service was over they started again, giggling a lot while they winked and pointed but he went away as quickly as he could.

He wasn't only shy. He was also a little bit frightened, because "being in love" was something that children were always teasing each other about — especially if the person they said you loved was ugly. It was a kind of insult. Felix was afraid of the boys having one more thing to tease him about.

But he couldn't stop thinking about the game that those two girls had played with him. He had thought of being in love with a girl before and he knew that lots of the children sometimes had sweethearts and would get friends to take secret love letters to them. But he had never dared to ask a girl to be his sweetheart because he knew that if she didn't want to she would take it as an insult and be angry with him, and if it was found out there would be a lot of teasing. That was why everyone who was in love tried to keep it a secret, at the beginning anyway.

There was one time when a girl had said "I love you" to him, but that hadn't been real. He was sitting on a wheelchair on the lawn reading when suddenly she ran up to him, a little ugly girl, with a fat face and short straight yellow hair, and she said it, hoarsely and quickly in his ear: "I love you." He could tell that she was just doing it for a dare and he reached out at her and caught her dress just before she turned to run away again, and the dress tore.

"Serves you right!" Felix had said to her.

But that was quite long ago, and the two girls who had teased him this Sunday at service time were big and pretty, and they had played this game with him because they wanted to and not because someone had dared them to. As he kept thinking about it, he began to feel nice instead of shy and cross. He began to feel excited that it was him instead of anyone else that those Daphne Ward girls, Florence and Dorothy, had chosen to tease.

The next service time Felix was sitting at the end of a bench where he could turn around easily and face the back of the playroom. When Florence and Dorothy were brought in he felt shy again, and sat with his chin and mouth resting on his hand, his eyes turned to the floor and his cheeks feeling hot.

It wasn't long before Florence began: "Oh, Felix! Hullo Felix . . . Don't you love me, Felix?" And Dorothy joined in: "Do you love me, Felix?"

Without lifting his eyes or moving his hand, Felix nodded.

"What! You do?" the two girls said, giggling, and Felix nodded again harder.

"Which one of us?" said Dorothy.

"Yes, which one of us do you love?" Florence asked as well.

Felix lifted his head to look at them then. Florence was the prettier one, but he said, "Both!"

They still talked to him in a sort of teasing way when they saw him at Service times, but that was because everyone around could hear, and he liked it because even though they pretended they were only playing at being his sweethearts for a joke, he knew that they really were. He wrote love letters addressed to both of them and got one of the "up" girls to take them to the Daphne Ward. And sometimes someone brought him a letter from Florence or Dorothy or both, and he felt very excited and happy.

Quite soon both the girls improved and stopped being bed patients, and not long after that Florence went home for good. So it was Dorothy Steenkamp, with her long brown hair and red cheeks, that Felix was left with as his sweetheart. He told her that she was the one he really loved.

"You said you also loved Florence," she reminded him.

"But I really love you," he insisted, "I really do." And it became true, so true that long afterwards, when she went home for good, he kept writing love letters to her for a long time, and when she came back one afternoon to visit her friends he was shivering all over with the excitement of seeing her again after months and months.

That was in spite of what happened in the meanwhile.

Dorothy let him go on being her sweetheart and everyone knew about it. He was always near her during the free hours on the lawns or in the playroom, and he was always sending her love letters with kisses and drawings of hearts. She never told him he had to stop, even when John began to be her boyfriend as well. Felix could tell, by the way they often held hands, that John was the one she really loved, and he knew that John saw more of her than he did. He felt jealous, but Dorothy said that both he and John were her boy friends and never told Felix to leave her and John alone. So the three of them spent a lot of time together, even though Felix felt that something was spoilt.

It didn't come right even though John went home for good and Felix had Dorothy to himself again. Still, he went on being in love with her. Her birthday was in autumn when the leaves of the Virginia creeper that covered The Home turned red or white or blotchy with bits of green, yellow, pink and cream. He thought of writing a special birthday card for her and collecting some of the nicest of these leaves and getting them stuck around the card to decorate it.

It was a Saturday morning and he was busy making his birthday love card at the table in the corner of the big playroom. He was alone at first, trying to stick some of the heart-shaped leaves on to the cardboard around his writing.

Then about six other boys came into the playroom. One of them was Harold Maggs, the biggest boy. He said to Felix, "What are you doing? Let's see . . . 'Dear darling Dorothy. Many happy returns of the day . . .'" The boys all laughed, then Harold said, "You know, you the only one of all the guys who's still got a girl friend. We all hate dames."

The other boys said: "Yeah, they're all lousy!"

"They stink!"

"You can't trust a woman!"

"Girl friends are just for sissies!"

"I've given mine the sack . . ."

"I sacked mine long ago."

Harold said, "You see! None of the chaps has a girlfriend, except you. We going to be anti-dames, but you're spoiling it. Why've you got to be different from all the other chaps?"

One of the others said, "Ag, he's just a sissy."

Everyone knew that Harold Maggs's girlfriend used to be Hughina Cortas, a Portuguese girl who was the prettiest girl in The Home — and the boys in Felix's dormitory used to talk about her and say that she used to go down to the koppie with Harold and hide in the bushes so that they could have digs. It was hard to imagine Hughina doing that, but exciting. It must be because Harold was so strong that he could make her do it even though she was scared of being found out. But she didn't tell on him, so that meant that she also wanted to do it — and that was the exciting part. (Somebody once told Felix that he should shake hands with Dorothy and tickle her palm with his bent finger turning around in a circle, and that would mean he was asking her for a dig — but he never thought that had anything to do with sweethearts, and anyway, he was frightened that if he did that it would make Dorothy cross with him.)

But Hughina had gone home for good quite long ago, and Harold had already had another girlfriend and given her the sack. But he never knew that he was the only boy who still had one. It was the opposite of the way things always used to be.

At first still thinking of the birthday card he was making, he didn't know what he was going to do. He always wished he could be popular, but he never was. The chaps were always saying that he was a Jewboy and a sissy and a professor and stingy, and would hardly ever lend him comics and things, and often teased him and (especially Harold) tortured him. Usually if they did things together they left him out. But now they were all going to be anti-dames, and they wanted him to be as well. If he wouldn't, he'd be a real spoil-sport.

Suddenly he knew. He said, "All right. I'll give Dorothy the sack!"

One of the chaps cheered, "Yay! Good old Felix!"

Felix looked around at all the boys' faces excitedly. Then he found the leaves and the cardboard on the table again.

"But I've made this card for her birthday . . ." For a moment again he didn't know what to do.

"So what! It's just a old dame's birthday," one of the boys said. "Smash it up!"

Then Felix said to Harold, "I know — I'll write her a hate letter, but first I'll send her this card so she thinks I still like her and won't expect me to give her the sack. That'll show that I'm really anti-dames."

Harold said, "Yes. That's a posh scheme. Finish the card and one of the chaps can take it to her."

And the other boys were saying, "Hell, hey, old

Jewboy's quite a sport . . ." "Congrats, professor, you're smart, hey!" "Oboy! Now we're *all* anti-dames . . ."

One of them helped Felix to stick the last couple of red leaves into place, and then they found a small girl and told her to take the birthday card to Dorothy. Another boy fetched Felix's exercise book with squared paper from his locker in the dormitory and all the boys stayed with him while Felix made up his hate letter, which Harold Maggs wrote down for him.

"You fat hippopotamus," it began — although Dorothy wasn't fat at all, "so you fancy yourself that I love you, but you're just mad because I really hate you like poison, you ugly snake . . ." The boys giggled all the time and laughed wildly again and again and patted Felix on the back and said, "Good old Felix!" Even Harold said, "Good old Jewboy, you can be a real sport when you want to!"

Suddenly Dorothy ran in through one of the doors of the playroom. On her way across to another that she went out by — while the group of boys at the table in the corner was suddenly quiet — she waved and smiled at Felix and said, "Thank you very much for the birthday card, Felix . . ."

It was a long time since she had smiled at him like that, as if they really were sweethearts.

As soon as she was gone the chaps laughed themselves sick because Felix's trick was working so well. And then Felix went on making up insults and finished off the letter, and told Harold to write

"HATE HATE HATE HATE" all round the edges of the page like a frame.

Felix heard that Dorothy cried when she got his hate letter so soon after the birthday love card. He hadn't thought that she might cry. And in the dining room or whenever they were in sight of each other, she turned her face away from him.

After a few days he asked one of the other girls to tell Dorothy that he apologised and that he would like to tell her something. Then when he saw her, he went to her and said that he was very, very sorry about the hate letter. He hadn't meant it — the other boys had made him do it. He hadn't meant it, he really still loved her. "So please, please, forgive me . . ."

Dorothy forgave him and let him go on again being her sweetheart in a sort of way. He went on writing her love letters and didn't stop for a long time after she went home for good. And on the day when he heard that she had come back for a visit, he shivered as if he was freezing as he made his way outside to where she was standing in her visitor's clothes in the sun.

Perfection

"You have to overcome the limitations of your self and supersede your passions. That is the road to perfection." There was something puzzling and frightening in some of the things Skipper Ross said. But Felix clung to them, because they told him that he was moving forwards again, and because of Skipper.

The war had been on for three years when Skipper Ross came to the Senior Home as supervisor of the boys. They were bad years for Felix. Though he had learnt to walk just a while before, his progress stopped now and he seemed to be fighting a war of his own. It was a war that perhaps had always been going on. But now, in these war years, he seemed to be losing, until Skipper Ross, the teacher of perfection, came to the rescue.

When he was small, if Moh was in a specially good mood she would gather him up and hug him so that he couldn't kick, saying, "Don't fight me! Don't fight me!" and try to bundle and tease him out of his tantrum. But usually she said, "I can't stand the sight of you when you're like this — just the sound of your voice gets on my nerves," her voice hitting and pushing him away. Only once was it her hand. He and Becky were quarrelling over a toy garden fork. He lost his temper, took hold of the fork and stabbed at Becky's back. As she squealed Moh's hand came down hard against the side of his head and knocked him off his knees.

One day Boetie Venter smashed the oxen that Sacred was making for Felix out of clay from the sloot, so Felix made Sacred walk him zigzag over the veld chasing Boetie. Waving a stick he yelled, "Run! Run! Sacred, make me run! I want to kill him! I'm going to catch you and kill you, Boetie, you devil! Run! Run!"

Sacred chuckled a little as they went along, and Boetie, keeping just out of reach, stopped after every little run to turn and stare, never looking as frightened as Felix wanted him to be. The chase went on until Moh came out on the veld and stopped it.

"It's not good for you to excite yourself like this," she said.

"Sometimes I believe," Moh said, "that it's all in your mind. You could do anything you wanted to if you really decided."

Felix heard the words "it's all in your mind" again one day when he was back at The Junior Home. He was in bed with a stomachache. Nurse Dell and Nurse Fourie were making beds in the dormitory and Nurse Dell was talking about an actress whose face was cut up in a car smash.

"She couldn't bear to let people see her, and all she wanted to do was die. Well, they got a lot of big photos of her before the accident and hung them on the walls of a room and they locked her in that room for six weeks with no mirrors. And that was her whole treatment. When she came out her scars had disappeared. Her face was beautiful, exactly the same as in those photos . . . That's psychology."

"What's that?" Nurse Fourie asked.

"Mind over matter," said Nurse Dell. "You see, it's all in the mind. I believe in it."

Mrs Fraser, the Standards teacher, who took both classes of the school for singing and exercises and Bible, sometimes made the children play a game called Control. For a whole minute timed on her watch, beginning from when she said, "Control!" everyone had to sit absolutely still except for breathing and blinking. Whenever anyone moved she called out his or her name and those who could walk had to get up and go to the back of the classroom. This was the hardest moment because you wanted to look at the one who had been called out — but even if you only turned your eyes, you would be called out too. The winners were the few who were left in when the minute was over.

Felix tried to hold every part of himself tight to stop it from wriggling, except his toes because they were hidden inside his shoes. But, every time, he was one of the first to be called out. At the end Mrs Fraser told him he had done better, or worse, than the time before. "Keep trying, Felix," she said, "you'll do it one day."

He knew that when he wanted to do something difficult he had to say to himself, "I can! I can!" After he had learnt to walk, he used to say it when he had a swing-door to push through, and when he climbed, with tiny pulling steps and long pauses, up the sloping ramp from bottom lawn. He said, "I can! I know I can!" when he had to pick himself up from the ground without a wall or tree or bench or something to pull up by — and at last he could. He was also getting to be steadier in his walking and falling less often, and learning to fall without hurting himself most times. Soon he would be ready to try climbing steps.

On cold or rainy Saturdays and week-day afternoons, when the children had to stay in the playrooms and boxes of toys and fancy-dress were brought in, they sometimes held concerts. One day Felix asked for a turn to act. In the funniest way he could, he introduced himself as Professor Mac-u-laff and began to ask a long, complicated riddle. As soon as he said, "Anybody who has heard this before, *don't* put up your hand!" the children all started to laugh. He tried not to laugh with them but he couldn't keep his giggles down. So he let go and roared and rocked and crouched at the knees, and the children roared back at his clowning. At last he could bob up and get his breath and say another couple of sentences which started another wave of laughter. By the time he had managed, in little spurts, to give the riddle and its answer, everyone was a little drunk from laughing so much.

After that he made a Professor Mac-u-laff speech at every concert the children held. Either they asked him to or he suggested it himself.

One day when Matron, during her afternoon round, sat on the willow tree seat and chatted with the children who gathered round her, she talked sadly about the extra lot of wildness that had been going on lately — disobedience, vandalism, ". . . and someone has even broken into your toy room, destroyed several beautiful toys and stolen a lot of others. Now I can't tell you how sad this sort of conduct makes me, because I know just how good my boys and girlies can be. Isn't that so?"

Some of the children chorused, "Yes, Matron."

Felix, who was still converted to Jesus, said, "But, Matron, I always try to be good."

And she said, "Yes, I know, Felix, you are one of my well-behaved boys."

But quite soon came the Sunday full of frightened feelings that even spoiled visiting time, when the war began between England and Germany, and about the same time Felix started getting into a lot of trouble.

Sydney was not one of the biggest boys but he was one of those who could dodge or run away when they teased someone. One day he pushed Felix over out of spite. Hardly hurt but shocked that anyone should make him fall on purpose, Felix sat on the path yelling as Sydney walked away. The next day he came to top lawn and saw Sydney sitting on the grass with his back to him. He dropped to his knees, stumped up behind Sydney and slipped his arm around his neck. "Got you!" he said, and began to bear-hug. "Revenge! Revenge!" he said again and again, squeezing more tightly as Sydney struggled and grunted but could not throw him off.

Children began shouting and a nurse, shouting too, came running up. She took hold of Felix by the waist and dragged him, shook him and slapped him until he had to let the softness of Sydney's neck slip from the crook of his arm.

"My God," she said, as Sydney rolled on the lawn coughing and crying, "he's blue in the face. You could have killed him."

Felix was disgraced. Matron scolded him very angrily. "I don't care what Sydney did to you," she said, "It can't excuse such wild animal behaviour. Now, Felix, I'm warning you, you have got to control your vicious impulses, otherwise you'll find yourself in a very serious situation indeed." He was sent to bed for a day with only dry bread and water and had to miss the next two treats the children were taken to. But for once he had punished someone who had done something against him.

When smaller boys sang at Felix:

> Valencia . . .
> Wie die hel

het jou vertel
'n Jood se piel
Is sonder vel?

he screamed at them, "Don't insult my nation!"
But with bigger boys he had to keep quiet because
they might get angry and remember that he was
afraid of being suffocated. Still, when Harold
Maggs stood over him and spat down onto his
head again and again, he lost his temper and for-
got to worry and screamed, "Leave me alone!
Leave me alone! You damn bullying devil!"

Harold Maggs laughed and said, "Shut up,
pipsqueak!" and spat again.

Jannie Malan, who slept in Felix's dormitory, was
one of the worst bullies. Felix thought of him
immediately on the night he half-woke to find
something terrible happening to him. He was
being pushed back into sleep, back into his pillow,
his head, half dissolved, rolling back into suffoca-
tion under black electric sacks. Jannie must be
doing something to him worse than any bully
had ever done. He thought he could hear a jum-
ble of voices talking and laughing. He tried to
shout, "Jannie, I'll get you for this!" but his own
voice only bubbled out of a mouth hundreds of
miles away from his spinning brain. Then his
brain buzzed and struggled in the dark until the
last crumb of it was smothered.

He was surprised to wake in the morning and
find himself unhurt. He said to Jannie Malan,
"What were you doing to me last night?"

"Me!" Jannie said. "I wasn't doing nothing to you.

Ask these ous. Ask Nurse Webster. Jirra, man! you
was having a fit."

Two months later Felix had a second fit, and then
others. He began to understand that this was
something that could ambush him from the edge
of sleep any night. It could get at him, as the
bullies could not, even when he was home on
holiday.

For a while there were no bullies to worry about.
Harold Maggs, who was a convalescent, not a cripple, left the Junior Home. Jannie Malan and two
others Felix was afraid of were promoted to the
Senior Home for older children along the ridge.
Roy Spencer, the strongest boy, liked teasing Felix
and testing his toughness, but he also liked talking about education and hypnotism and *The
Wonder World Book*, so they were friends. Felix
was one of the top boys.

But he was nearly fourteen and one day Matron told him that it was his turn to be promoted
to the Senior Home. Everyone knew that the Senior Home had visiting every Sunday and you were
allowed home for a week-end every month and
there were many more treats. But now that Mrs
Fraser had retired, the two Homes shared one
school building, so Felix knew what some of the
Senior Home boys were like. He begged to be
allowed to stay where he was, but Matron said,
"I'm sorry, my boy, it's rules. We can't have great
big chaps growing up among the little ones. Besides, it's for your own sake, too, big man. It's
time for you to move on in the world."

The Senior Home was a new brick-faced building with steel windows and flat roofs like boxes. The inmates called it "jail". There were special rules to keep them in control and the Matron was strict, but they were not watched as closely as at the Junior Home, and in their dormitories and common room and the hidden corners of the grounds and at the swimming pool, the biggest boys, especially Willem Prinsloo, were really in charge.

During his first holiday Felix asked his parents not to send him back. "I'm not happy there," he explained, and only after many questions did he admit, "There's a lot of bullying."

"That shouldn't be allowed," Moh said, shocked. "Surely the nurses can put a stop to it."

Dad said, "Tell me the ruffians' names. I'll give them a choking off, the loafers! Anti-Semites, I suppose. I'll tell them what for. I'm not afraid. What are their names? They'll leave you alone in future."

"No, Dad, don't do anything," Felix begged. "They'll punish me . . ."

"Punish you! The bloody cheek! They're the ones who'll be punished, don't you worry. Of *course* I must do something. Come on, tell me who they are . . ."

"No, I asked you *please*, Dad, please, please, *please*!" Felix shouted. "Don't do anything! It won't do any bloody good . . ."

He gave no names, but Dad told Matron about the bullying and she lectured the bigger boys and after that things were worse. Felix had known they would be, because whenever a bully was caught by

a member of staff he always got out of it by saying, "I was only playing with him," and if he suspected there had been a complaint, the splitbek
would be in for the bully's revenge. A splitbek
was the worst thing a boy could be. Now that the
big boys knew Felix had split on them (even though
he hadn't told any names), they not only teased him
for fun because he was weak and had a temper,
and despised him because he was Jewish and a
show-off at school and scouts and one of the use-
less ones who were too slow to go on errands and
couldn't make their own beds — they hated him
for splitting.

Felix was shouting, "Down with Hitler!" when
Willem Prinsloo came past.

"What have you got against Hitler, pipsqueak?"
Willem asked.

"He's the worst man in the world," said Felix.

"Ag, kak, man!" Willem growled. "Come on,
what have *you* got against him?"

"Well, he wants to kill all of the Jewish people."

"That's just propaganda," said Willem. "Anyway,
what did he ever do to you?"

"He's killed lots of my people already."

"Your people, who? Your father? Your auntie?"

"No . . ." said Felix. "But I think he's got some of
my father's relations."

"You think he's got . . . Well, I didn't ask you what
you think. I asked you what did he do to *you*?"

"Nothing . . ." said Felix.

"So? Why do you just talk what you don't know?
Do you know what the English did in the Anglo-

Boer War? They killed thousands of Boer women and children — they let them nearly die of hunger then they put poison on their food. So, don't you talk kak when you don't know about something. I say down with England up with Hitler! Show me your hand, Jewboy!   Let's see if there's hair growing in it . . ."

"There isn't," said Felix.

"Well, look out! If you toss yourself off, hair will grow in your hand and you'll get mad. If I ever catch you I'll moer you, you hear!"

One evening all the boys and girls were gathered in the dining room for a bioscope show. But something went wrong with the projector, so the boys' supervisor, who was in charge, asked those who had any talent to entertain the audience to make up for the film. After a few others had performed, Felix went up and did a Professor Mac-u-laff act. Everyone laughed wildly all the way through, even the staff members who were there, and afterwards, as Felix was going back to his chair, the supervisor called across to him: "Felix, have you got your Entertainer's Badge?"

"No," said Felix.

"Well, you should have," said the supervisor.

There was something more than this that kept Felix gasping as he struggled, during the rest of the concert, to squash down the laugh that was boiling up in his stomach. It was the way Willem Prinsloo had laughed as much as anybody and called out, "Hey, the Jewboy's not so bad!"

He was popular for two days. Then one morning

in the bathroom someone saw him using his facecloth to wipe the matter out of his eyes. "Sis! is that the way you wash?" the boy said, and told everyone about it. So again the big boys were all disgusted with Felix.

"You've got to get in the water *some* time, Joodjie." Felix was surprised that Willem cared what he did. "I'll hold you safe. 'Strue's God on my scout's honour, I won't leave you loose. You've got my promise in front of all these okes as witnesses."

"If there was a tube for me to just lie on . . ." Felix parried.

"No, man! I'll take you in safely. I want to help you . . . What's the matter, Jewboy, are you so shit-scared of water? Or don't you trust me? I've said 'strue's God. Are you calling me a liar?"

"No, no!" Felix said. "All right, I'll get in."

Once they were in the water, Willem pried Felix's clutching hands loose and locked them in one fist, then pressed his other hand on his head as though to duck him. Felix knew it was probably a bluff to tease and test him, but he screamed and struggled until Willem took him out. In the changing pavilion Willem said, "Sies! but you're a real coward, you know? You're nips like a kaffir."

"I know," Felix said, shivering.

For two years he was frightened, because he never knew when something like this, or worse, was going to happen. One day someone might pick him up and throw him into the swimming pool. Someone might stop pretending, just to make him squirm, and really push a hot cigarette against his skin. Someone might pull a blanket over his head and tie it at his neck. Willem and some of the others seemed dangerous enough to kill you if they could do it without being found out. He was scared all the time, and ashamed of the things they despised him for (except being Jewish).

Whenever a new boy came everyone wanted to be his friend. Edwin Shaver looked very interesting. He sounded clever and he had lots of things, a typewriter, a watch and books. But though he was not able-bodied, he spent most of his time at first with big boys or with members of staff to whom he was always talking in an important way, using lots of long words. When someone tried to bully him he began shouting and throwing whatever he could reach and after that he was left alone.

Everyone began to respect Edwin's will-power, though some of the boys said he was stuck-up. He seemed to do whatever he wanted to without getting into trouble even if it was against the rules. He marched into the kitchen, which was out of bounds, and ordered the cook to give him a piece of bread and jam or a glass of milk.

One evening, just after cocoa time, he walked through Felix's dormitory. Felix suddenly threw his empty mug after him and shouted, "That's a mug for a stuck-up mug!"

Edwin whirled around. "And what, may I ask, was that all about, impertinent child?" he said, glaring at Felix, with his chin and nose lifted high.

"It's just not fair," said Felix.

"I don't know what you're referring to, dear boy," said Edwin, turning away, "but all's fair in love and war . . ."

One day when Felix had been teased, frightened and hurt until he cried, he went and leaned against the fence at the edge of the garden and stared down the koppie. Looking at the nearest roofs of rich houses, he thought of all the people inside and all the things they were able to do. They were worrying about Hitler and Up North. If only they knew what was happening to him so nearby, he was sure they'd do something to stop it, the way they phoned and complained when fruit was pinched from their trees or when stones landed on their roofs. If only they knew, they'd want to stop it, he was sure.

When the Senior Home first began to have a supervisor for the boys in their spare time, there was a new one every few months. The first one organised gardening on the koppie and was always explaining about humus and compost. Another one believed in astrology and took the nickname, Pluto. The next one was Sarge van Tonder, who was out of the army because he had been injured Up North. He lectured the boys about discipline. Then came Mr Gascoyne, who smoked a pipe and talked about courtesy ("When you see a lady off at a tram-stop, you should slip her exact fare into her hand to save her having to hunt for it in her purse").

Skipper Ross wanted to teach the boys to strive for perfection. He was a soft-voiced man with silver hair and a young clean face. He was a plumber by trade and had played football for Scotland. Felix was interested in anyone who had done anything international or famous, but he soon had another reason to like the new supervisor.

Every day at first Skipper Ross called all the boys together for a discussion, but the only ones who enjoyed listening to him and tried to answer his questions were Edwin Shaver and Felix. So Skipper began talking to them alone whenever he could. It was the first time that a staff member paid special attention to Felix.

A thought is a thing. Anything you believe or imagine or wish will be manifested. You can make coins appear in your hand out of thin air. A maimed man can grow a new leg. You can have anything you want if your attitudes are positive. You can have perfection.

"What are positive attitudes?"

"Saying yes, not no. Fixing your thoughts on what you want, not what you fear. Seeing what there is to love, not to hate. Turning the other cheek . . ."

"And what is perfection?"

"Allowing God to express himself through you, the way Christ did."

"But I'm Jewish."

"What kind of difference should that make? Jesus is only one example. There are Masters of Life in every time and country."

Soon after Skipper came, Willem Prinsloo and three of the other worst bullies reached the top of the school and left the Senior Home. Now there was no one for Felix to hate or be afraid of, and he knew that just by not hating anyone and believing in himself, he was learning to use the same power that Skipper said the Masters of Life used.

There were also exercises to be done whenever you could, like straightening clenched fingers one by one, to train concentration and will power and control, or complete relaxation of the body inch by inch to let the healing forces flow through. There were powerful words to say to oneself morning and night, like, "Day by day, in every way, I am getting better and better." There was faith to hold on to that you would get the things you wanted. There were thoughts of love and healing to beam out to everyone around, because whatever one gives out comes back to one.

"And it must be true," Felix told anyone who would listen — Skipper, Edwin, Moh and Dad when they visited. "I know it's true, because I've been feeling so happy since I started doing it."

One afternoon at the end of rest-time the word went around, "Old Willem Prinsloo's come on a visit."

One of the smaller boys said, "Ooer God! I hate him."

"I'll tell him you said so," another said, teasing.

"So what! He isn't a pupil any more. He can't

touch any of us."

"All the same, I bet you still scared to cheek him."

"Ah, well, he was the biggest bully. Every guy was scared of him."

Sitting on the lawn and listening, Felix found his breath coming fast and his throat feeling tight. "I'm going to," he said.

"What?"

"Cheek Willem . . . I'm going to take revenge on him."

"Ag, you'll never."

"What, *you,* little Jewboy . . ."

"Just wait till he comes," said Felix.

"Hey, you chaps, come and listen here . . ."

In the next few minutes a lot of boys gathered on the lawn and stood watching Felix. At last Willem came through the door from the long dormitory. He was wearing a jacket and a tie and he began shaking hands with some of the boys. Suddenly Felix yelled, "Hey, you, Willem Prinsloo!"

Willem turned and stared at him. Felix almost could not go on, but a small boy near him giggled, and he stared back at Willem and yelled even louder, "How do you feel now that your bullying days are over? You can't touch any of us now, you know! You're a visitor, not a pupil any more. You're not so big when no one's scared of you any more, hey?"

More boys were giggling and Willem looked too surprised to speak or move. Felix went on yelling cheekier taunts and insults, until Willem jerked around, shouted over his shoulder, "I'll see you tomorrow at the police station, you hear!" and stalked away without another word to anyone.

That night, for the first time since Skipper had come, Felix had an epileptic fit. When he saw Skipper next day he told him about it.

"Aha!" said Skipper, "I'm not altogether surprised at something like this. Now, what is it I hear about you and the old boy who came to visit yesterday?"

"Oh, do you know about that?" Felix hadn't wanted Skipper to know.

"Yes, I know that you treated him very unkindly."

"Well, he used to bully all of us . . ."

"I've heard about that," said Skipper. "But don't you see that after what you did it was natural for you to have a fit?"

"Why?"

"Well, revenge is always negative. Your thoughts and feelings were poisonously negative, so they poisoned your system and produced a negative result, a fit. I've told you that everything that happens to you is produced by your own thoughts."

Felix nodded, and Skipper went on, "Now, I'll tell you what I want you to do. You're to write this boy a letter asking him to forgive you." It was the first time Skipper had ordered Felix to do something.

"Oh . . . But he . . . I . . ." Felix began. Then he saw that it was the only thing. "Yes, Skipper," he said.

"Go and do it right away. I'll get his address for you from Matron."

"Yes, Skipper," said Felix. When he had written the letter he handed it to Skipper to post and said, "Thank you for showing me what a positive attitude really means. I'm sure I'll never have another fit."

"I'm also sure of that," said Skipper.

Felix told Skipper that he wished he could start a school magazine, and Skipper said, "If you're clear about it in your mind then it is already in the process of coming true." A few days later he told Felix that he had spoken to Matron about it and now she and the chairman of the committee agreed that if Felix would edit it, the office secretary would duplicate it.

Felix's first Editor's Chat in *The Hilltop* was about the thought that had become manifested on the material plane as this magazine.

"It's time for me to move on to something new," Skipper said. "I believe you were the main reason I was sent here. Now that you have an understanding of truth, you can go on seeking and do what you have to do on your own."

"What do I have to do?" Felix asked.

"You have to win self-mastery."

"But, Skipper, I still need you to show me how."

"You know the essentials, you can move on your own. In any case, I'll still see you and write to you, and I want you to keep me in touch with your progress."

After Skipper left, things remained very different from Felix's first two years at the Senior Home. The worst bullies were gone. Felix had no more fits. He was friends, almost best friends, with Edwin Shaver, and they discussed mind-over-matter, planes, astral projection, hypnotism, self-hypnosis, yoga and psychology. Edwin had many ambitions, and Felix believed him when he said he would achieve them all.

His own first ambition had been fulfilled with the starting of *The Hilltop* and everyone, even the committee members, knew he was the editor. And now that he could sit safely in the common-room for hours, he started writing a novel called *The Fifth Limb*. (It was about a girl who lost a leg and became bitter and hopeless, cutting her hair short and wearing ugly clothes, until she met someone like Skipper who taught her about positive attitudes . . .)

And there were Skipper's wonderful letters, which explained more and more of the truth, told Felix the names of books he should read and reminded him that he had something important to achieve ("and remember, just as giving is receiving, so preparing is achieving").

Moh, Mavis and Becky went to Durban on holiday that July, so Felix spent the month with Skipper and his family at a tea garden in Ferndale that Skipper was managing. Mrs Ross was so wise and calm and their two adopted little girls were so good-natured and beautiful that it seemed as if everything around Skipper was special. On two evenings he took Felix with him to a School of Mind lecture in an auditorium in town. Felix wrote to Moh: "The lecturer was a very powerful speaker, but I knew nearly about everything he told us from Skipper already. He is like a wizard and Mrs Ross is like a kind angel and it is like being in paradise here. They are vegetarians. I am very happy and learning new things every day. I don't even miss being home for these holidays."

Felix gave a farewell party at the Senior Home. None of the inmates ever did that, but it was Dad's idea. "After all," he said, "you had your schooling here for nothing, except a donation of a few pounds I gave here and there. You grew up here . . ." It was strange having Moh and Dad at a party at the Home. In the middle of it, in a funny shy way, Dad made a speech about "taking stock". Felix knew all the boys hated speeches and were only listening to the Jewish accent, not the words. But they were getting an extra party for nothing so they couldn't mock, and when Matron said, "Three cheers for Mr and Mrs Greenspan for giving us this lovely party — hip-hip!" they all cheered loudly. Then they sang "For he's a jolly good fellow" and gave three more cheers for Felix himself.

While Felix was waiting for classes to start at the college where he was going to do his matric, he went to stay with Skipper again for a fortnight. They went to School of Mind lectures given by a visitor from England named Dr Amery who had spent two years among the Masters of Life in Tibet. Skipper said that Dr Amery was probably evolved highly enough to be a Master of Life himself by now. Felix felt sure that Skipper, even though he hadn't been to Tibet, was one too. Afterwards Skipper fetched him from home to go to several more of Dr Amery's lectures and healing sessions.

Moh and Dad were always grateful to Skipper for having Felix to stay or taking him to lectures. When Felix described School of Mind, Moh said, "Oh, I believe in it. I'm sure it's in your mind to make something wonderful happen. If Mr Ross helps you to do that, I'll . . . I'll believe in him forever . . ."

Because he knew Skipper's reasons for not eating meat, Felix wanted to be a vegetarian, but Dad said, "Don't be foolish. You've got to eat properly. Do you want to spoil your health?"

"But it is healthy to be a vegetarian," Felix said.

"You don't know what you're talking about. You've got to be very strong to be a vegetarian. Don't I know with my own brother. Uncle Lewis was a vegetarian for two years, and then how sick he got and what the doctor said to him: 'You dare not,' he said to him, 'you dare not' . . ."

"But I'm not Uncle Lewis," Felix shouted, losing his temper, and the argument went on until Moh screamed, "Stop shouting, both of you. I can't stand it when you carry on like this. If only Mr Ross would teach you how to control your temper, I'd say he was the greatest miracle worker."

At the college, which was four classrooms and an office in an old building in the middle of town, it was a long time before any of the boys and girls talked to Felix. He watched them, especially the pretty girls, and listened to them, especially the boys who told each other rude jokes and described adventures with shopgirls and nurses.

During the mid-year holiday he went again to stay with Skipper who was now living on a small farm past Pretoria that he was managing for a welfare organisation which wanted him to turn it into a home for problem boys — only Skipper said, "No boy is a problem until you think he is one."

He had a lot of driving to do in his small truck, to neighbouring farms, to nearby shops or in to town, and Felix often rode with him. Skipper talked about the secrets of proper driving, as he talked about the secrets of whatever he had to do, and he began to let Felix hold the steering-wheel while he drove. Soon Felix found that he could not only keep the truck straight on the road but could sometimes turn a corner without Skipper needing to touch the wheel. After some longer drives, his hands were blistered because he had been gripping the wheel so tightly. But he said, "I'm sure I could learn to drive by myself."

And Skipper said, "You know very well you could."

On the farm Felix stayed close to Skipper while he finished building, flooring and plastering a circular brick wall which, with a pipe from the nearby borehole pump leading over the wall and an outlet pipe from a hole at the base, became a dam. When it was all done the pipe from the throbbing pump spurted, GUSH-trickle-GUSH-trickle-GUSH-trickle, and the new dam filled with clear water. The sunlight flashed from the ripples and shone through them, carrying dancing nets of light and shadow down to the floor and walls.

"Water is a very spiritual element," Skipper remarked as they gazed at it. "There's meaning in those patterns, I'm sure, if only we knew how to interpret them."

In the same way, he went about his other work, turning an outhouse into a dormitory, making a fence, directing the African workers in ploughing fields and fertilizing them for green peas and tomatoes and mielies and asters. All the time, through talking about tools and nails and wood, about bricks and cement, about pipes and the pump and water and soil, he was teaching Felix more about the Truth.

"You really should do some physical work every day, some gardening or wood-chopping or painting, or even sweeping a floor if there's nothing else. There are three things every man should do in his life, plant a tree, build a house and have a baby. That doesn't always have to be an actual child. It can be some dream, some plan, some work that you are really concerned in as your very own. Your first baby was *The Hilltop*, but you must also plant your tree and build your house."

"But how, Skipper?"

"You know how very well. We've talked about it

often enough."

Felix pondered. "I must act as though I can . . . is that right?"

"Exactly. Because it's true. You really can do anything at all, if only you will recognise your real self instead of holding on to the false idea of yourself you have had all your life!"

Nodding slowly, Felix said again, "Act as though I can . . ."

In the matric examinations Felix and Edwin Shaver both failed History and Afrikaans. They couldn't understand how it had happened. Nor could Mr Franklin, the principal of the college, so he applied for a re-mark, but the result was the same. Dad was sure their papers must have gone astray because they had written in a separate room, using typewriters and being allowed double time. But later, after Felix disgraced himself over Mavis's pretty Christian friend, Marjory Cane, by waiting for her in the veld near her flats and asking her to let him have a dig — Dad said, "How can you expect to pass your exams if your mind is full of evil thoughts when you should be concentrating on your studies . . .!"

Felix wanted to write the sups in March, but Moh said it was too much of a strain on him, and Dad agreed. So he couldn't try for university. The principal told Dad about the literary editor of a magazine who could give Felix private lessons in short story writing.

The tutor's name was Mr de Waal and he had a way of laughing enthusiastically whenever he liked anything Felix wrote or said. He began training him to observe things carefully and describe them realistically. "It's only life itself that can teach you the stories that are worth telling," he explained. "You can't be didactic, you must let life speak for itself."

When he began to feel less uncomfortable with his shame about Marjory Cane, Felix wrote to Skipper about it. "Why," he asked, "do I have to perform miracles of suppression?"

Skipper replied, "Suppression is a negative idea. Just remember that sex can be sublimated into great spiritual powers. I hope you will come to stay with us again soon. It may be very important."

In July that year the literature lessons were interrupted when Felix went to stay with Skipper while Dad, Moh, Mavis and Becky went to Warmbaths on holiday. It turned out to be by far Felix's longest visit, because toward the end of the month a message came to Warmbaths from a neighbour at home to say that burglars had ransacked the house. So the family cut short their holiday and, instead of picking Felix up on the way back, left him to stay on with Skipper while Moh was putting the house in order again.

"It may be for the best that this has happened," said Skipper. "I think there are good reasons for you to stay on with us for quite a while."

Felix had brought with him *Palgrave's Golden Treasury* and a novel, which Mr de Waal had recommended him to read, and his typewriter so that he could keep up his writing practice. But Skipper had more than ever for him to do. Felix had to get up before dawn — not sunrise but the real dawn that woke the birds — and do exercises on the frosty grass. He had to practise digging the earth with a pick and shovel, even if the weight almost made him fall. He had to practise moving bricks; he had to lay a brick. He had to sit on the broken black turf of a ploughed furrow, that was like sharp stones, and slide along planting a row of mealie seeds. He had to practise moving mud with a hoe so that water from Skipper's dam could irrigate a new furrow. Skipper taught him how to work the clutch, gears, starter, accelerator and brakes of the truck, and he really drove a little by himself on the farm. And there were important books on Skipper's shelves that it was time he read — though one must not get lost in reading matter.

They were reminded about the books by Edwin Shaver, who also came to stay on the farm for two weeks. "I'm determined to investigate every aspect of occult thought and power," he said.

"All truths are part of one truth," Skipper remarked.

"Precisely, precisely!" Edwin agreed. "I want to know all the parts and so comprehend the one central truth." He sparked off very thoughtful discussions in the evenings when they sat before a log fire in the grate. Once he pointed out in a book a picture of a meditating yogi who was willing the snake of his sexual energy to mount up his spine to his brain.

"As I understand it, this diagram symbolises one of the most esoteric mystical techniques of the East," he said.

Skipper nodded. "It's the sublimation of sex into spirit force. It can be done other ways, but I believe all the Tibetan Masters of Life have tapped their powers in this way."

"Fascinating," said Edwin. "Once I've mastered astral projection, I'm going to concentrate on this phase of yoga."

When Edwin had gone, Mrs Ross remarked, "Edwin really is amazing, you know. I wonder why he chooses to remain disabled."

"Yes, it is interesting," Skipper agreed. "With that terrific will power of his he could be healed tomorrow — and he knows it."

"Chooses . . .?" Felix asked.

"Oh, yes, obviously he chooses it. Everyone chooses what they've got. Your karma is only what you've chosen consciously or unconsciously by the way you've lived, in this life or in a past one."

The discussions now, in the evenings, between the firelight from the grate and the lamplight from the table, and during the day whenever it was possible for Skipper to talk as he worked, were more about how Felix himself ought to live.

Every week or two Felix 'phoned home or the family 'phoned him.

Moh said, "How long do you want to stay away?"

"There's a lot I have to do here. Skipper wants me to learn everything."

"Are you happy?"

"Of course."

"I'm missing you." Moh laughed, "I miss our quarrels."

"I don't miss those," said Felix.

Skipper had bought himself a plot near Halfway House. Once or twice a week he went there for the day to build rooms and a tiny dam, mend fences, lay pipes and furrows and plant an orchard. Depending on what had to be done, he took some of the Africans from the farm to help him or he went alone with Felix. Once or twice Mrs Ross and the children came as well and they had a picnic lunch.

The orchard was planted on a bright but fiercely cold windy day. Six big petrol drums were loaded on to the truck and the Africans, dipping and hauling buckets over the wall of the little dam, poured and poured until the drums were full of water. Then Skipper, with Felix beside him, drove over the bumpy ground, the water slopping and splashing into the spiteful wind, to the holes that had been dug for the young trees waiting with their stripped tops and bandaged roots. Now the buckets were dipped into the drums and three bucketfuls hauled out and poured into each hole.

Everyone was splashed wet and bitten by the wind on the bare piece of veld. Seeing a half-filled bucket left on the ground near the truck, Felix got down from the cabin of the truck, and began to drag the bucket, a few paces at a time, towards the nearest dry hole.

"I had a dream last night," Skipper said one

morning to Felix, "concerning you. It left me with a strong feeling that you are ready for something important."

"Oh?" said Felix. "What is it?"

"Well, that's up to you," said Skipper, "you know what you've been preparing for . . . Now I think you should not come with me to the plot today but stay here and think about things. Meg and the children are going in to Pretoria, and I'm taking the boys with me for the second half of the orchard, so you'll be alone and can get quiet and concentrate your thoughts. What do you say?"

"All right, Skipper," Felix said, nodding slowly, "I'll stay . . ."

"I believe I'll find something wonderful when I get back. Great unseen powers have been gathering around you."

. . . close to something important . . . what he'd been preparing for . . . something wonderful. It could only be bodily perfection. But today? So suddenly! And by himself, alone? But how? What must he do? How do you perform a miracle?

All morning Felix walked, to the farm gate, to the end of the ploughed fields, to the double row of bluegums, and sat for long quiet spells to rest, and all the time he walked and sat he thought about everything he had learned. The only way he could find out what he had to do was by thinking it out, thinking harder and deeper than ever in his life.

The secret name of God: I AM. I am God – omnipresent, omniscient, omnipotent. My thought fills the uni-

verse. Its reality is already there. It only has to be manifested on the material plane. I only have to believe for it to visibly happen. Believe what? Believe perfection. But I am perfect. I have been perfect through eternity. I am God. What must I do to make it physical?

The thoughts went round and round, catching up another and another truth, putting the whole universe into a clear, beautiful pattern of logic. But hour after hour there was no answer to what must be done today. How must he make the truth show through in his body?

In the early afternoon he lay on the grass patch against the farmhouse and concentrated on inch-by-inch relaxation. Memories came to him: *I must act as though I can . . . I must visualize the perfection I desire and manifest my faith in its reality by acting as though it was already there. Preparing is achieving. I must act as though I can . . . I must hold a picture of my perfect self clearly in my mind . . . I see myself running, jumping, dancing, laying bricks, digging with a pick, climbing a tree, driving a car, swimming . . .*

He sat up and looked toward the dam. Swimming. Perhaps that was the way to manifest his faith and make the miracle happen. He must throw himself into the dam affirming that he could swim. With everyone away from the farm he could not be counting on any outside help to save him from drowning. His rescue must be inside himself. He would be relying on his own inner power, which was the power of the universe, set free by his act of faith, to make him swim. And that miracle would bring with it the revelation of his whole bodily perfection.

He walked to the dam. There was a mound of earth and stones piled over the outlet pipe. If he stood on it he would be high enough to pull himself over the wall into the water. First he would half sit on the edge of the wall, then swing a leg over and pull with foot and arm against the inner curve and fall in, shoulders first, back down. He visualised himself tumbling into the water, sending up a splash and waves, turning over, rising and swimming, more and more strongly, gracefully, swiftly, across the sixteen feet of the dam and around its circumference three times, then reaching to the top of the sheer wall, hauling himself smoothly out and running, in his perfect body, across the veld to the house.

That would be the miracle. Yes, of course. This was what Skipper had left him here to discover, what he was waiting for today. This was what Moh had always been waiting for. The miracle that, all alone, here now, only he could perform. Yes. He thought it through again as he stood staring into the cloudy greenish water, trying to follow the blurred patterns of light and shadow that slid across the bottom of the dam between jagged flashes of light and fragments of his own reflection that bellied away on ripples under the breeze. Yes, that was the thing he must do.

He climbed the mound and stretched a hand down to the water. He could just reach. He splashed a few times, multiplying the ripples.

"I can't," he heard himself saying. "Oh, hell! I can't . . . My faith isn't strong enough. Skipper! Skipper — I'm sorry . . ." He drew his hand quickly back, clambered off the mound and walked as fast as he could back to the house.

After a while he went to the telephone. "Moh," he said, when he heard her voice, "tell Dad to come and fetch me, please — soon. I want to come home . . ."

Almost an Idyll

At the Rand Easter Show Felix was on his way to a hall where, he had read, there was an exhibition of famous paintings. The hall was on the far side of the dusty grounds, beyond the Tower of Light, high up on a terrace. He was footsore and had a headache. His face was hot and bundles of the afternoon's slanting sunrays seemed to have got caught onto everything he looked at and poked at him from every direction. He held one hand on top of his ruffled head and narrowed his eyes and pulled back his mouth between a grimace and a grin. Every vista in the spaces between the displays rippled and rolled with the movements of the crowds. The air was filled with an uneven roar of mixed music and many voices.

Suddenly he stopped noticing the scene, stopped walking and took his hand from the top of his head. At the far side of the drive he was going along he saw a refreshment stall. And one of the three aproned women serving behind the counter was Marjory Cane. He stood for a minute or two staring at her and, breathing hard, he began at last to walk on; but after three steps he turned, quickly crossed the driveway and entered the shade under the awning of the refreshments stall.

He asked for an ice-cream, and while waiting kept his head down, but cast glance after glance at Marjory who was slicing up a loaf of bread. When he was served he moved along the counter until he was opposite her. She finished cutting up the loaf and piled the slices on a plate. Then at last she turned. She was looking at him. He stared back stiffly for a moment. Then his face twitched — and he smiled at her over his ice-cream. And Marjory smiled back, with an almost conspiratorial smile. It was that, even though it was kind and forgiving as well.

At seventeen Felix had come home for good, to the house on the fringe of the half-built suburb, next to the stretch of naked veld. It began at the fence of the house, a space of tall grass mixed with khaki bush and snakeweed, black-jacks, wild dandelions and long-thorned bushes with yellow berries.

In the past two years, whenever he had come home for school holidays, Marjory had been there. She was Mavis's best friend, and this meant that she was always in and out of the house. She came with them to bioscope matinees and picnics, and sometimes Mavis even brought her along when the family went to visit an aunt on a Sunday afternoon.

But only a week or two after Felix finished with the Senior Home, there was a quarrel between Mavis and Marjory. They would not speak to each other, Mavis stopped going to the block of flats around the corner where Marjory lived, and Marjory no longer came to the house.

Felix was now at home in the new, half-built suburb of neat small houses, whose bare red streets all ran straight and ended, nearly every one, in the smoky khaki of the wild grass. Marjory Cane, also, was orderly, obedient and useful, and yet had something in her, too, that was untamed. She was always busy, running errands, taking care of small children for mothers who had gone to town, and yet, through her usual primness a strong mischief would suddenly flash, and it filled him with the same sense of promise or threat that he felt when he was about to take a walk across that stretch of veld.

Going to that picnic, during his last holiday, as the five or six of them had trooped, drawing him in his box-cart, down the narrow beaten footpath that twisted through the grass, Mavis and Marjory had walked ahead whispering together and giggling. Then suddenly Marjory turned to the others and demanded, "What does V.V.V. stand for?"

She had hardly given them time to guess:

"Three V's!"

"Victory, victory, victory!" Then she bent and drew three V's on the pathway with a twig, in such a way that they looked like a naked woman. She had rubbed them out again with her shoe almost immediately and she and Mavis, laughing uncontrollably, ran ahead to the shade under the line of planted bluegum trees..

When Felix and the others came up to them Marjory was tucking her dress up. She had kicked off her shoes and done cartwheels and splits for a while on an odd patch of grass that was flat as a lawn. Chattering, joking all the time, she flung herself down on a rug and lay near him sucking an orange. He remembered a riddle he had heard at The Home and was about to speak when she jumped up and commanded another boy to help her up into the bottom branches of a tall tree. And she had gone on climbing until she was rocking about in the thin branches near the very top.

"Yoo-hoo!" she called. "Yoo-hoo! Mavis! You can't see mee-hee! Felix! Sam! Yoo-hoo! Sah-ham! You can't see where I am!"

The boy Sam, shouting back, began to climb after her, but she came down out of his reach and ran far across the grass towards one of the sloots, vanishing over the edge among the bushes with Sam behind her.

Felix sat listening to the calls and laughter rising from the sloot, the book he had brought along, hoping to read aloud to them all, lying on his lap unread even by himself. And he thought about that riddle he knew. He could ask her, because she had been a Girl Guide and knew the Morse Code.

"What is dot dot dash?" he would say.

And she would reply, "Dot dot dash is U!"

"No," he would say; and he would show her another way of drawing a naked woman, with two dots and a dash. But he decided he would ask it only of her. It would have to be when he and she were alone somewhere, and not in front of anyone else. That had been the beginning of the idea.

But it was only later that he started to be sure of what he wanted: after the time she had been sitting next to him on the sofa making copies of the rhyming clues that he composed for the treasure hunt. He made up his mind that the next time she sat next to him in her shorts, sharing the secret of his clues, he was going to put his arm around her waist, and touch her thigh . . .

But there was no next time. A few days later Marjory and Mavis had their quarrel and became enemies, and Felix had to do his watching from a distance.

But although her voice rang like a churchbell from down in the veld where she nursed the flat-babies for their mothers, or from up the street where she called a greeting to someone, or demanded "Gangway!" for her bicycle, he dared not approach until the summer of his homecoming was gone and the next winter had almost followed it. He realized, as the memory of the glint of Marjory's thighs dimmed in the pages of his books, that she was locked away from him — or rather he was locked away from her — locked in with his studies, his books, his chess . . .

He was locked in with them even after he had done with college and even when, as he did every day, he put away his book and fetched his floppy canvas hat and walked out along the thin footpath through the grass and black-jacks and long-thorned berry bushes. He would go a good distance across the open space to the raised rocky place beyond the three clay-sloots, and there he would stand and stare across at the white block of flats with the row of garages behind. He hoped to see the gilt flash of Marjory's hair as she crossed the yard. Sometimes he even hoped that something would bring her running down into the veld along the footpath towards him, alone. Or else he would wait at some place near the flats where she might pass — in a sort of ambush which he always deserted before she came. But in any case she would never come alone. She was always with girls and boys, or with babies to nurse.

It was a school-day in August, a morning that seemed to have run ahead of spring, bright and warm. The wind lay low and left the white dump dust in the cracks and corners where it had been etched yesterday. The streets were still and sleepy, shaken loose from the net of noise that the children always flung about them.

And on his front verandah Felix sat reading, half aware each time he looked up from his book, only of a sort of desolation. But suddenly it was different. There was Marjory, with a basket, walking up the street to the vegetable shop. She had not gone to high school to-day. She was not in her school "gym" but in a bright green dress that set off the color of her hair.

He stood up to watch for her to come out of the shop. At last she came down the street, calling, "Hullo, Felix," as she passed. He replied in a choked voice and watched her turn the corner on the path to the flats. He stared for a long time at the point where she had vanished, with his heart thumping, his breath out of control and his thoughts whirling. At last the real opportunity had come. This time, when he laid his ambush she would walk into it. They would be face to face and he would speak to her. And he was not sure of what he would say.

He went indoors to tell Moh he was going for a walk, because it was such a pleasant morning. He took from her meekly the floppy canvas hat she handed to him. Then he went out into the thin clear sunlight and down to the edge of the space where it burned without shadows on the strong, grey grass.

He leaned against the wall of one of the garages and waited.

Perhaps nothing would bring her out of the flat again for hours . . . Suddenly a dog ran from the other side of the building, barking at his feet. He nearly fell. Then that kitchen door opened and Marjory appeared with some letters in her hand for the post office.

She was trying to take hold of the dog's collar. "It's all right, Felix," she was saying kindly, "he doesn't bite . . . Go home, Chuckle! Down!"

"No, he's all right," he mumbled weakly. He wished he had not worn the hat. "Marjory," he said at last. "Marjory . . . will you come with me to the sloot?"

She looked puzzled. "*Why?*"

"Or the garage . . . The garage . . ." he stammered. "What?"

"I . . . Will . . .? Let's . . . let's have a dig," he said at last, breathlessly.

Marjory's eyes opened wide and she gasped a huge gulp of air. "Felix!" She hurled his name from her as she turned and ran away on her errand leaving him staring blindly into the grass that shivered beneath the gathering heat of the sun.

It was done! In his mouth he kept tasting his impossible words. And the echo in his ear, again and again, of her gasp of reproach. It was the sun, he told Moh hastily when he got home; it had been too hot outside, that was why his face was flushed. But hours later he could still feel the heat of his cheeks.

Late that evening he was sitting alone in the kitchen, sipping the cocoa Moh had made him before going to bed, when Mavis came into the room, having just returned from the monthly dance at the school hall. "Felix," she said, "did you see Marjory Cane to-day?"

He gave a kind of leap. "Yes," he replied after a moment, in a choked whisper. "How do you know?"

"She told me at the social." With a look of revulsion and anger Mavis turned and ran out of the kitchen. He could drink no more cocoa. He was lost now, altogether, and there was nothing left for him to do but to hang himself.

He went to his room and after drawing the curtains he stood for a few minutes twisting the strong green cord around his hands. Then suddenly it occurred to him that he had a choice. He did not have to escape; he could face up to what he had done by telling Moh and Dad about it.

Spring came. The first rains sent up the strong aroma of wet earth, and shades of green and yellow began to wash over the khaki of the veld. Sprouts of green stabbed through the spiny black clumps left by grassfires. Along the new avenues the twigs of the railed-in saplings were spotted with green; their leaves began to unfold.

But it was more than a season before Felix could face his parents without his cheeks turning red. It was even longer before Mavis's eyes lost their power to make him feel that an icy wind had suddenly risen. It was years before he could hear the name Marjory — even over the radio, or innocently read from a newspaper — without a guilty start. But worst of all was the echo, still ringing in his head, of her exclamation of his name, and the memory of her look of disappointment.

Every afternoon before spring was over, he began again to take the old walk across the veld to the high, rocky place beyond the sloots. He stood there as though he were waiting for a glimpse of Marjory moving about the block of flats. And yet if he saw her in the street he would turn aside; and if she passed the verandah where he sat reading he would keep his head down and pretend he did not see her.

One day she stood speaking with some friends in the street within view of his window. He stared out at her, his face pressed to the pane, wondering why she had chosen to stand on that corner, expecting her to turn suddenly and look at him. And when she was gone he could not get out of his mind her gestures, her dress, and the sound of her laughter.

All this time he felt like a sleep walker. It was

summer when he discovered with a gradual shock where he had been straying. Only then did he come to understand why it was that when he was alone he whispered Marjory's name to himself over and over again. He had found something that could heal all the rawness left from the rude contact of that day. But, he wondered, how was he going to give it to her? Again and again when she seemed near enough he hesitated — not because of shame but because, once more, he did not know what he must say.

But now, eating his ice-cream at the Rand Easter Show, suddenly he knew exactly what to say. As soon as his breathing became quieter and he felt he could speak, he would smile at her and say her name, and then lean towards her across the counter.

But when he raised his eyes Marjory had taken off her apron and was folding it up. She came from behind the counter and joined another girl, who was waiting for her. They moved off and in a minute they were swallowed up, the colours of their dresses vanishing in the crowds.

While he finished his ice-cream Felix felt that the people all about him were not real and he was standing there alone. But no, it was not that . . . it was the grass. He thought suddenly of the tall silvery grass that had grown on these heights during the centuries before the city had come. Through the pavements, under the buildings and the feet of the people, a kind of ghost of all that grass was still flourishing, still rustling under the dry elastic autumn air. He hadn't told Marjory he loved her.   He knew the words now, but even if he could run it would be impossible to find her in the crowd.

A Right Time for Trams

When he was fifteen Felix had been told by Skipper Ross that a man's life is the embodiment of his thoughts. After that, he often conjured up an image, which grew more detailed as the years passed, of a young man heroically perfect, poised, graceful, strong, limitlessly capable. Himself, he asserted, himself.

It was this image that was suddenly wrenched out of his reach — while a different one, which he had not called up and could not suppress, obtruded in its place — the first time he heard the sound of his own recorded voice. The recording machine belonged to his cousin whom he and his parents were visiting. They were making little speeches which, his cousin said, he wanted to keep on the tape, a vocal snapshot album. Felix took his turn at the microphone eagerly. "Friends, Romans, countrymen, lend me your ears," he began, "I come to bury Caesar, not to praise him." And then, partly because it struck him that he was being pretentious, partly because he was not certain of what came next, he broke off and giggled, muttering, "Oh, hang! Sorry . . ." and hastily handed back the microphone.

He listened in a tremble as the tape was played back, and when he heard his own voice he was shocked. He had expected the gauche, undignified performance. It was not that, but the voice itself, a throaty, breathless blurt, dense as the lowing of a nervous calf. And the enunciation was thick and sticky (had he paused so long there? and there? and had he gulped like that there?) with the dragged syllables ill-defined and half lost in the blur of noise. That was how he spoke. It was idiot-like, brutish. He had not known that beyond the occasional stammer he sounded like that.

When the recording machine gave him this outsider's insight into his condition he was eighteen years old. It was weeks before he could begin to take comfort from remembering that he had been excited facing the microphone and his breathing had been out of control. What he had heard was a half-choked distortion of his ordinary speech. Normally he did not sound nearly as bad as that. Months had to pass, though, before the memory became dim and he could begin again dutifully to conjure up the old image and believe in it.

As he dwelt on it as before, it became clearer and more insistent than ever, until one strange evening when, as though to put his vision to the proof, he forced himself to go alone to the tram stop near his house and board a tram unaided for the first time in his life.

Giddily triumphant, he rode to town where he alighted amid brilliance and bustle and, after losing his sense of direction and nearly being run over, found his way to the Colosseum too late to get a seat. Then he took another tram home. So he set himself free to come and go about town and the suburbs as he pleased.

"Of course! Of course!" exclaimed Mr de Waal meeting him one day — in town. "There's really nothing you can't do — hey? in your own good time." He smiled. "In fact, I suspect that what you are doing is just choosing your own time for everything. I can't think of a better age to start riding trams than nineteen. Before that you can't appreciate it." Felix laughed with him. He did appreciate tram-riding. In a tram he was on his own, a stranger among strangers. A drunken man might sit next to him, or a dubious woman. He was making contact with real life.

There was even more triumph in the tram-riding a few months afterwards when he became a student and could go up to the university every day for lectures. And at university, the first to detach herself from the formidable mass of students that confronted him, was Bathea. Until then he was more bewildered than triumphant in the class rooms and corridors where the seventeen- and eighteen-year-old students, stridently sophisticated, kept their distance from him, as though his extra years made him, not older, but too young for them. Bathea was in his English and History classes. Although she was a girl with a reticent manner, hers was the first gesture of recognition Felix received from any of his classmates.

He saw her near him in the tram on the way home

one afternoon after three weeks of classes. She gave him a hesitant smile and asked, "Do you live out this way, too?" To his responsive enquiries about her courses she replied very briefly, with blush and stammer, as though he had caught her out, or had touched the embarrassed reluctance with which she seemed to carry her own body. The whole encounter was rather painful. But the next day she was friendly and sat beside him through a lecture. And afterwards, though he half expected her to shy away forever from some wrong move on his part, they spent more time with each other than with anyone else at university.

This provided relief for him from being alone — but more than that it gave him the wonderful pleasure of being chosen by someone, like all those lucky partners he saw around him. This was all there was to it for the rest of that year, except for a time of wild but serious questioning and dreaming. There were always secret thoughts, wishful thoughts which he knew had to be ignored, dismissed. But Bathea clearly liked his company. She felt at home with him, enjoyed his conversation. Was it just that? Could it mean more?

The possibility filled him until, going one day to join her at the tea break on the crowded sunny front steps of the main building, he found her laughing at the banter of a senior science student whom she introduced as Paul and who took her to have coffee with him. Or rather, until later — for though after that he knew she was often with Paul, he felt her no different towards himself —

until Mavis told him that she had seen Bathea at a dance with someone of Paul's description.

Because it was Bathea, this meant something. He couldn't imagine her (even with the friendship they had) being willing to come out with him for an evening. That she went with Paul — who behaved in a genially protective way toward her — meant that he must, at least a little, be loved by her. Felix felt a pang of envy and a small despair as one wild hope receded. But soon he was glad of his new certainty: Bathea's friendship was simply itself. He could see clearly, and would always be cheerfully able to give, the sensible contained acceptance it required of him.

In the campus arts festival held early in the second half of the year, Felix won a prize. This earned him some attention and he made several new friends and so saw much less of Bathea outside their classes during the remainder of the year. But midway through the year-end vacation, while Bathea was away at the coast, he read a newspaper notice that Paul was engaged to be married to a girl named Julia Feinberg.

Felix did not see Bathea until the day they went to register for the new year of study. "Hello," she greeted him. "It seems like ages and ages."

"Yes, it does," he admitted. "What was your holiday like?"

"Oh, it was a dream." Then "You didn't go away, did you? I wish you'd been down there. That's all it needed."

He could see no sign of pain and realised that

though it was new to him, the end of whatever had been between her and Paul must be months old to her. She was in gayer spirits than ever — as he found when they took coffee together after registering, and she told him about her holiday. And this was something that didn't wear off altogether with her holiday sun-tan. He did not feel any more, as he had at first, that she was turning to him as a sort of refuge from the world. He was at first surprised that they re-established contact so smoothly after their long estrangement. Then he became aware of a new element in her friendliness.

It wasn't merely that now they saw more of each other outside the university — that she visited him at home for an afternoon now and again, that she invited him with other friends of hers on a Sunday evening every month or so to listen to music at her house. He marvelled at the naturalness of her acceptance when, drawing on the confidence he had learnt from his new friends, he invited her, for the first time, to see a play with him. "We'd have to travel both ways by tram, of course," he reminded her.

"Do you think I'd consent to go any other way?" she teased.

She took it all as a matter of course. But for that very reason it was a kind of miracle which left him pondering. What was its nature and what were its limits — this friendliness she so matter-of-factly gave to him? For a while this questioning was confined to the interstices between the excitements of another relationship, but by the middle of his second year that particular dream was over.

Constantly now he scrutinised and weighed everything Bathea said and did. He found, and repeatedly found, meanings more wonderful than he had thought he could ever expect. It seemed it was possible, he told himself one day, that Bathea loved him. Could this be why nothing had come of her relationship with Paul? For his part, in love with the love he guessed at, he had to acknowledge himself not only attracted, as always, by her kindness and beauty, but now passionately in love with her.

Once surprised by his own boldness, he had named these feelings to himself, trying to push them out of his thoughts. They were frivolous fancies. Though he felt what he called passion he knew he could stifle it if he had to. Then could it be a passion at all — a real passion? And if his own feeling was so questionable, how could he ever know what hers was? But though he could ridicule the thought of his being loved, he could not forget or, in the end, deny his loving, and he let it silently fill him.

In love with her he saw more vividly the reserve, the inaccessibility he had sensed in her from their first meeting. Like the delicate petals of the white magnolia, she was not to be touched. He could enjoy her loveliness, and accept the impossibility of anything more.

But suddenly, as though at the flick of an electric switch, everything changed. One day as they came from a classroom in which he had presented a short paper, Bathea said, "You read beautifully, you know, Felix."

"Me?" he cried. "Read beautifully? You don't mean that. Do you? Do you?" But he had heard in her words the voice of total acceptance, and that was the one that counted.

The tensions between Mr de Waal's illuminations of literature and the strictures of the English Department had been growing for Felix since the start of his course. Late in the second year, he broke off his studies. Disappointed, his father found him a job of sorts in the office of the family business.

Felix and Bathea telephoned each other now and again, and occasionally he took her to a film or a play. But it was chiefly at her Sunday musical evenings that they saw each other now. Her other guests were all sophisticated professional young people who, between the symphonies and concertos, discussed politics and science and art. It was as though they set up their own reality — isolated in the darkened drawing-room, choosing and changing records, listening in reverential silence, making polite jokes and having earnest discussions at tea time — it was an ideal reality for them, sensitive, clear-eyed and well-informed as they were — one in which all uncertainty and all passion were suspended out of the flesh and transmuted into music.

Although he participated pleasantly enough in the conversations, Felix felt as if he were outside the bell-jar that contained Bathea and her friends. He hardly heard the music he sat through in order to be near her, but, silenced and covered in darkness, he was overwhelmed again and again by the rising waves of his own passion and uncertainty. From the street and the sky would come hardly enough light to let him distinguish between furniture and people, between men and women, between a girl he had never seen before and Bathea reclining near her on the floor. But he knew where she was and his eyes turned to her increasingly.

At one of these evenings, while a record was being changed, Bathea startled Felix by beckoning to him to come with her out of the drawing-room. He joined her in the passage. "Oh, Felix," she said. "Be an angel and do me a favour." She explained that she had invited a new guest whom she did not know very well. "I don't think he expected this kind of music. He seems to be having a miserable time. But I think he's interested in books and films, so please when tea time comes won't you talk to him and make him feel a little more at home?"

Felix said that he would try. Then he added, with a grin, "Though I may not really try hard enough."

"Why not?"

"Well, jealousy. What's he got that we haven't got? Would you go to so much trouble for your other guests?"

"Oh, sir," she said, dropping a little curtsey, "your every wish is my command."

He chuckled and went back into the room with her. He wanted to cry out to her but he knew such a cry would shatter the bell jar and he was terrified of the consequences. At the same time he was curious about them.

The jar finally cracked without a blow from him. He had come to a party given by a friend from university and found Bathea there escorted by one of the regular guests of her musical evenings, a young barrister named Louis. She was looking especially lovely, so much so that everyone must be aware of her and although she was very warm toward Felix he felt her to be more inaccessible than ever.

Wandering about the house late in the evening, he came to the kitchen to find her sitting at the kitchen table with Louis who had obviously just been sick on the floor. He was drunk. Bathea was wiping his face and forehead with a moistened handkerchief, stroking his head. For her sake Felix was filled with anger. How could anyone be so insensitive, so clumsy as to subject her to this disgusting embarrassment? He marvelled at her goodness in showing no sign of annoyance with Louis.

She looked up, relieved to see Felix, and asked him to try and find a sheet or two of newspaper for the floor. He went to do so and when he returned she was cradling Louis's head on her shoulder. Felix spread the paper and then Bathea said, "Stay with us until he feels better." So for more than half an hour Felix sat in the kitchen and chatted with her.

Louis lay with his head in her lap, one arm dangling on the floor. He seemed to be asleep. But soon his hand rested on Bathea's foot. She ignored it. As Felix watched Louis's hand suddenly pushed up over her knee, under the hem of her skirt.

Bathea pushed Louis's arm away. "This isn't the time or place," she said, and shoved Louis upright until he flopped forward again on the table. "I'll go and see if I can get him some black coffee," she said, getting up and going out..

Felix sat a while staring at the young man, who still seemed to be asleep. Louis must, he thought, be blind drunk to treat Bathea in that way. But still that caress could not easily be dismissed. Hadn't Bathea's own re-jecting of it contained an acceptance? What of other times and other places? What if there had been no witness? Everything he believed about Bathea was suddenly fluid and he rocked on a swell of thoughts and feelings until he felt the dizzier and more helpless of the two in that kitchen.

At last he left the room, but in the passage he met Bathea returning with some cups of coffee. "Where are you going?" she asked. "I've brought you a cup too. Stay with us. We'll give you a lift home."

He followed her back to the kitchen and watched in silence as she held a cup for Louis to drink, then when the muzzy head sank down on to the table again, her name forced itself between Felix's teeth which seemed locked together as though he were very cold.

She turned toward him. "Yes?"

"Nothing," he said, "nothing." Then, as her look became questioning, he rocked his head and smiled. "Oh, I don't know what—I'm sorry, Bathea.

It's just thinking aloud. Just nothing."

During the following days his will could hardly hold the rushing of his thoughts round and round in an obsessive whirlpool, but again and again, "Nothing, nothing," was the answer he tried to force on himself. On the fourth evening, he came suddenly to a decision, and almost immediately he went out of his house and took the tram to Bathea's neighbourhood. He rang her doorbell and after a long time she opened to him.

"Felix, it's you," she said. "Come in, let me close the door."

"Sorry, sorry," he said, as he came in. "Should have phoned first. But I . . . I . . ."

"Is there something the matter?" she said.

"Bathea," he heard his voice sounding as if from far off, "I couldn't wait any more. I've got to talk to you, tell you something."

She pressed her lips together. "Oh, Felix," she said sadly, "has it got to, got to be now? Someone is picking me up for a meeting in about five minutes and I'm not even dressed yet." He saw then that she was in a dressing-gown.

"Oh," he said. "Sorry. It's my fault for not phoning, finding out."

"Can't you just say what you want to now?"

"No, we must talk. Another time . . ."

"Yes," she said, "I'll be home tomorrow afternoon. Is that all right?" He nodded. "I'm so, so sorry, Felix. I want so much to talk. It's such a pity, but I can't do anything about it."

"Of course," he said. "Of course." He turned to the door. "It's all right. Tomorrow will do perfectly. I'm sorry for just bursting in." He went out.

Tomorrow afternoon. Yes, he would return then, and then he would tell his love and claim her love at last. That was settled. The tryst was made, and in merely making it he knew that at last he had sent the screening glass shivering and tinkling around them. The biggest thing was done already. He had only to live through the hours to the answering moment.

He was as restless that night as he had been every night since the party. When morning came he was vague and tense, feeling the weight of the hours ahead of him. When he arrived in town he found he was late for work. Still he stopped on the way to the office — glad to make himself a few minutes later — and went into a jeweller's and bought a brooch. He did his work like a somnambulist, with no purpose but to reach the distant lunch hour, after which he was not returning to work. But at one o'clock he was still not free to start his journey. He did not want to descend on Bathea immediately she arrived home. He would come about half-past two, she should be ready for him by then. He still had nearly an hour to kill. So though he had no appetite he went into a restaurant and tried to eat something. Then he followed a long, roundabout route to his tram terminus. He walked the last few blocks with a growing eagerness that left him hardly aware of the streets, the lunch-hour crowds, the open square he had to cross as he came near the City Hall.

". . . This poor cripple who is dragging his way past us will illustrate that great difference." A raised, emphatic voice brought it to Felix as sharply as a slap on the cheek that he was walking between a pavement preacher and the people waiting in a queue for a tram, at whom he was directing his sermon. "Yes, my friends," the man was shouting, "I would ask you to look well at this unfortunate man, and I would ask you to at the same time think of the souls of those who know not Christ."

Felix turned angrily to glare the man into silence, but the parable would not be cut short. "Oh, my dear friends, I can tell you that in the sight of God those unfortunate sinners are worse afflicted in their souls than this poor fellow is in his crippled body." With the voice reaching after him Felix moved on as fast as he could to be out of the range of all those curious eyes. For a while it was indignation at the preacher's stupidity that boiled in him, but then this steamed away and he was left weak and disheartened and filled with an old horror.

He went to a telephone booth. "Bathea, I've changed my mind," he blurted when he heard her voice. "You'll think I'm mad, but please, I'm not coming after all this afternoon."

"Oh. Well, all right Felix, I won't see you then."

"I'm sorry," he said. "I had a very stupid idea in my head. Something brought me to my senses."

"I see. But perhaps it would have been better if we had talked about it."

"No," he said quickly. "No, I'm sure it's better that we don't." Then he added, "But why? Do you know what I wanted to say to you?"

"Yes, I think so."

"How — When did you find out?"

"I've known for a long time, Felix."

"I see. But what would be the point of talking about it?"

"Well, if there is something that worries you perhaps we can make some sort of arrangement about it."

"But what? We couldn't arrange for you not to be what you are."

"Ah, Felix, no. But I think we should arrange not to see each other."

"Oh, I see," he said slowly, and was silent.

"Don't you think it would be best?"

"No, why? Why? Nothing is different. You knew before what I felt. You said you knew all along."

"Yes, Felix. But I thought you . . ."

"What? You thought I what?"

"No," she said. "It doesn't matter. It's nothing."

"You thought I was realistic?"

"Something like that."

"Yes," he said. "I haven't been. I know that now. I'm sorry. But please believe me, it's not necessary to change anything between us. I'll manage better now that I've seen things clearly."

"I hope so. We've been such good friends. But Felix, if you ever feel that it would be better for you not to see me any more, I'll understand."

"All right," he said slowly. "All right, Bathea. Good-bye."

"Good-bye, Felix." He heard her ring off.

He must have known all along that this was exactly how it had to be in spite of the perversity that had led him to dream and hope otherwise. The impossibility of what he had been imagining was also, like her friendliness, a thing to be taken for granted. How far he had got from the truth about Bathea (much, much further than Louis at the party), about people, above all about himself! He put the telephone down at last, left the booth and went out into the stony bleakness of the street over which the parching sunlight poured.

It was plain to him now at last what the reality was for him, what the facts were that he had to live with, and they would never again have to be dinned into him as the street preacher had dinned them. The dream he had woven about Bathea must be stripped away, forgotten for his safety. Perhaps even Bathea must be forgotten for his safety, and she was right about their not seeing each other. What he was facing now was all that was rightfully his.

When he had taken his seat on the tram — in which he was only going home now and not to Bathea — he felt in his pocket the little box with the brooch he had bought that morning. At its touch, he felt no access of bitterness — but a curious lifting of his mood. He looked about, at the people near him in the tram, then those out in the busy street: a news vendor, two tramway pointsmen, school-children with their satchels and suitcases, a pretty girl.

He followed her with his gaze as she walked: tracing the tilting glints in her hair, the swell and sway of her hips from the stalk of her waist, until she was out of sight. Now he understood why he was brimming with a kind of glee. In his mental picture of what, so mistakenly, clumsily, futilely he had tried to do, he could see nothing he was not glad about.

Special Arrangements

Matthew came from the ticket office, smiling. He said unnecessarily, "Wait here for me, will you?", veered off across the crowded foyer and went into the manager's office. After a while he emerged with the manager and pointed Felix out.

Felix mouthed a protest, but Matthew was still busy explaining. Felix moved toward him. "What is this? Are you arranging aisle seats, or something?"

"Yes. They had none at the box office, but it's all in order now."

"Matthew, I don't . . ." Felix began, but Matthew was giving one more word to the attendant at the door of the auditorium to make sure that the correct instruction was passed on to the usherette.

Matthew turned to the girl with the torch: "Will you walk more slowly, please. My friend . . ."

By the time they were seated and all the trouble was over, it no longer seemed worthwhile protesting. Felix muttered to himself, "But I don't need an aisle seat." To have said that to Matthew now would have seemed ungrateful.

Their friendship had begun not many months

before, and was the first important result of Felix's conquest — that is how he thought of it — of the avenue that ran past his house and linked the city center to the airport and the world outside. On the fiercely triumphant evening of his first lone tram ride, he had set himself free to make his home not just the house and a few suburban streets, but Johannesburg at large.

It was a timely emancipation. Mr de Waal had put an end to his writing lessons, declaring that he had nothing more to teach him: "You have to learn the rest on your own, through writing and reading, and through life." Felix was trying to work regularly and had earned his first couple of guineas from a magazine. He felt ready to extend himself, to make new beginnings. Dad allowed him £3 a month as pocket money. He drew up a list of the books he thought he should own and brought it to a bookshop near his tram terminus.

The shop assistant read through the list in silence. Something was amusing him. "Do you know what all these could cost?" he asked at last. "Assuming we had them in stock."

"I didn't mean to get them all now," said Felix.

"I should think not!" The assistant gave a snort of laughter. "These would cost at least a hundred pounds. Are they for yourself?"

"Yes."

"How many of them have you read?"

"Only two or three, and parts of some others . . . But they're all good books, aren't they?"

The young man laughed aloud. "Oh, yes, they're good books, most of them, the classics! What did you say your name was?"

By the time Felix left the shop with his first few purchases the assistant had answered a number of other questions and the feeling of a friendship had begun. A few days later Felix came to the shop with a pocketful of his typescripts, and Matthew in his turn presented him with a grey booklet he took from a pile on one of the shelves.

"With my compliments," he said, then took it back and wrote inside the cover. "To my friend, Felix, with kind regards, Matthew Kahn," and on the outside, "OVERTURE — 39 poems by matthew kahn." With his elegant accent and slight neat figure, he looked to Felix like the ideal poet: finely made and self-possessed.

Felix gasped his thanks. "When was this published?"

"Only last month," Matthew replied with a broad shy smile.

"And who . . .?"

"Oh, of course there are no poetry publishers here. I had it printed myself."

"And is this," said Felix, noticing the dedication, "the Mary Fotheringham whose stories are published in the *Monthly Review*?"

"Yes. Mary. She's a very old, very close friend of mine."

"She's been in my mind only lately," said Felix with some excitement, "especially because of that last story they had. It's exactly the kind I've been trying to write."

"Well, I'm sure she'd be pleased to know you admire her work. Why don't you write and tell her? I'll give you her address."

In the tram going home Felix read some of Matthew's poems, seeming to hear his precise, energetic voice.

> The night's scent stains
> my fingertips
> when your well-dark hair pours on my thigh.

It seemed important writing. Carrying the book along with Mary Fotheringham's address and the sense of Matthew's warmth, he felt quite loaded with treasures. And that set a pattern. Matthew had a great store of treasures: acquaintances, books and journals, music, paintings, places, ideas, and he set about sharing them lavishly.

Felix accepted this with an extra sense of privilege when he noticed that with most people Matthew was moody and aloof. He seemed barely to tolerate both the owners and customers of the bookshop and even his own parents; life, for him, seemed to be an extremely delicate affair for which most people were far too coarse. Felix felt flattered that Matthew had singled him out — but often rather uncertain since he suspected that the texture of Matthew's mind might be too fine and subtle for him as well as for most people.

Once Matthew made one of his sudden surprising little self-revelations. (He preferred such strokes to direct explanations of himself.) He pointed out an overgrown corner of the park near his home: that was where, as a small boy, he had had sex play with a little girl friend. "Oh," he laughed, "when I think how innocent we were . . . so innocent! So innocent!" The comment was mysterious to Felix. His memory edged darkly toward and away from an ignorant tense encounter with a little girl cousin far back in his own childhood. He was awed by Matthew's poise which turned the confession into something almost poetic.

By Matthew's light all sorts of things became unexpectedly poetic, or unexpectedly coarse, ridiculous, wrong. Felix never knew when he might bring down Matthew's friendly bantering scorn for some lapse of taste or naïve opinion. Once when they were dining together Felix refused buttered bread with a meat dish. "We don't keep kosher, but we just never like mixing milk and meat," he explained.

"Oh, but I must say," Matthew warmly jeered, "you are a hypocrite, my friend, such a hypocrite!" Felix did not know how to defend himself.

He supposed that in each of these mystifying moments Matthew was pointing some lesson for him. But incidents such as the one at the cinema made Felix puzzle over his friend's odd little actions. Matthew was quite free in questioning him about his wants and needs in larger matters, so it was curious that he should not have asked him whether he needed an aisle seat. Perhaps his kindness, like his high spirits, sometimes burst impulsively and clumsily forth. Or, Felix supposed, the uneven moments would all reveal their special good reasons when he got to know Matthew better.

The college principal and Uncle Lewis had used their influence in high quarters and Mr de Waal had contributed a testimonial — the result was that Felix was required to take only one oral examination to be exempted from rewriting the matric. Matthew was away on a visit to Europe when the last of this business was finished and Felix faced the issue of going to university. Mr de Waal had sometimes joked about the limitations of intellectuals and university education. But now he declared that, all the same, a few academic years could do a writer no harm, and, more important, university was an experience. To Felix it was a longed-for experience. He applied, and after several interviews was accepted. His first year of study was the year he turned twenty-one.

University as experience conjured up an image of things done with friends. But at first, besides the forbiddingly fragile one with Bathea, he made no close new friendships. At the same time, the daily nearness of so many pretty girls renewed his sense of being remote from the fulfillment of some of his keenest wishes. He stared hungrily at them, especially when they relaxed, sometimes indiscreetly, on the steps before the Greek portico of Central Block.

It was only after he had gained an identity, by winning the story competition of the campus Arts Festival, that he began to make many friends. And on Rag Saturday early in his second year he began a kind of apprenticeship in love.

He went that morning to the parade ground in town where the floats were assembling for the procession, and wandered among the rag-tagged lorries, enjoying the hectic atmosphere as the students in their fancy-dress did last minute jobs of hammering, stitching and painting, armed themselves with money boxes and guided their floats into the procession line. A threat of rain heightened the excitement; through the clouds all that showed of the sun was a pale glow, hard to find. The first few lorries had maneuvered across the grounds and roared slow-gearing through the gateway, into the street and toward the heart of town, when he heard, "Wouldn't you like to join our float?"

The speaker was up on one of the lorries. He recognised a girl he had often noticed on the campus, not resting on the steps but darting along corridors, foyers and pathways, strikingly dressed and very lovely. Now she was wearing black slacks and a black sequined blouse. He indicated his drab raincoat.

"I'm not dressed for it."

"That doesn't matter. I'm not either," she said. "Come on. There's even a spare money box for you."

"Well, okay," he said, held by the warmth of her urging. "Why not, just for fun?"

She called, "Oh good!" and made three men help him up on to the lorry. Her name was Janine Dorman and she knew his without his telling it. As the float passed through the gates and began to roll between straggled lines of spectators she was saying, "I've seen you often and thought you were Felix Greenspan, but I could never get to meet you."

"Why didn't you just come and talk? I wish you had."

She smiled. "Well, I don't know . . . You might have been a stern sort of person." They were turning a corner and caught their first glimpse of the main crowds that had turned out to greet the Rag parade.

"Stern? Oh, gosh . . .!" He laughed. "Do I look it? And even if I was, I'm sure nobody could be so stern that they'd object if you talked to them."

"Well, thank you for the compliment . . . But, oh, I wish . . ." her look was suddenly grave and her voice low — "I wish you wouldn't say things like that before you know me properly."

"Am I going to know you properly?" he asked in wonder.

"I hope you want to," she said, as they came into the midst of the crowd which cheered and waved and tossed a rain of coins onto the passing float. In the softened light that filtered through the grey stir of low cloud, the tall buildings stood out. Their ledges and windows were crowded with spectators, and the buildings themselves seemed to lean and press forward as if they were also part of the audience. The noise, the pleased acclaim, even the numbers of the watching people, seemed magnified by this eager pressing close of the inanimate city and the sky. Felix felt that he had been plunged into the exhilarating centre of everything.

But it was not the intimate autumn weather that was evoking this feeling, nor even the triumphal ride through town. It was this girl, who had snatched him up, as though by design, to celebrate him with her ardent glances, her air of rescuing tenderness, her dense-fleshed beauty, as full of promise as the clouds were full of warm rain. She was pointing the whole hot beam of her attention onto him, and he was dazzled.

When the procession ended she was joined by a friend. "We want to see the ballet this afternoon, if we can get in," she told Felix. "Won't you come with us?"

"I thought of doing some reading for varsity."

"Oh, it's the weekend. You can do it tomorrow," she said, as though reading weren't endless and could make room for other things.

"And today's Rag Day," the other girl said. "Nobody does any work."

"Come with us," Janine urged. "Or don't you want to?"

"I do. I'd like to very much."

Janine brought her palms together with a clap. "Hurray!" she shouted, smiling as though he had made her a gift.

It was a world famous company of dancers that they saw, and this was the first professional ballet Felix had seen. But as though she had made it and possessed it, he saw that stage as only an extension of Janine, another view of the world she was admitting him into. Later he saw in it the keynote of the following weeks. The wonder of things burned in him like a fever while she kept him within her orbit, immersed in her lavish atmosphere. On the campus he was now one of the centres of her activity. She would run up when she saw him, with a look not only of fondness but somehow of relief.

She had just been given her own black Citroën which she dubbed Lalapanzi, and it served not only as the vehicle by which they went on their outings, but a sort of center of their communion. They talked while they drove, and often continued, unable to break off, for many minutes after they had arrived at their destination. Always, she fed his wonder and pleasure by seeming to find wonder and pleasure in being with him, as they talked and talked, exploring and explaining, as though this were the last knowledge they might ever learn, the last communication they might ever make.

One evening, as they reached the door of a new place she was taking him to she asked with no warning, "Felix, do you know me?"

He returned her earnest smile, but felt bewildered. "I know a lot, Janine, but I feel there's still so much for me to learn."

She gave him a look of warm gratitude, as though it had been a different answer to a different question.

But his answer, affirming her mystery, was for him a sort of crying out. So far they had never even touched each other's hands, and for the time being he had enough to enjoy in her mere intense closeness and all the untested possibilities it implied. He knew he must not rush things — did not know how to rush them, or move them at any pace — but surely the tumescence of desire and ignorance was about to be lanced, he was about to enter the heart of life and manhood and reality.

He had been seeing less of Matthew Kahn — who

had returned from Europe early in the same year
— than in the days before university. But whenever there was an opportunity, Matthew displayed
the same generosity and interest as before, and in
time, inevitably, Felix told him about Janine. Matthew listened judiciously.

"Are you in love with her?" he asked at last.

The boldness of the question made Felix hesitate,
but the glamour of that word, that simplification,
was more than he could resist.

"Yes."

"And does she love you?"

This was more than he dared to claim. "I don't
know."

Matthew sat inscrutably musing. Later he clapped
Felix on the shoulder. "You know, I'd very much
like to meet this girl of yours," he said, laughter an-
nouncing a switch of mood from his first thought-
fulness. "Will you arrange it?"

Felix, held for a moment by a reluctance to make
Janine a subject of scrutiny, paused before answering, "Well . . . If she's willing, yes, of course."

"Oh, I'm sure she'll be willing," Matthew said.

And when Felix had given Janine an account of
his friend and his request, she said simply, "I'd like
to meet him."

An appointment was made for a Sunday afternoon. Matthew, driving his little Morris, first fetched
Felix, who guided him to the building where Janine
shared a flat with two other girls. The weather was
fine and tender, with sunlight broken and softened
by small white clouds, and as she emerged from the
building Janine applauded: "Oh, what an absolu-

tely beautiful day!"

Felix suddenly felt and slightly feared her innocence, and was surprised that he had never thought of her that way before. Matthew responded easily, "Yes, a perfect day for where I'm going to take you."

"And where's that?"

"Oh, one of my favourite spots," Matthew said, ushering her into the car. And he added two or three times, "A most delightful place, just you wait and see."

It was the Bird Sanctuary, which neither of them had seen before. The woods, the fields, the waters, the birds themselves and even the weather all seemed to have come together in a special state of fresh quiet loveliness at Matthew's command. Apart from them the place was almost deserted, and their own personalities and poised relationships seemed to infuse the scene and determine its character for that day. After their walk they rested in a little rustic shelter, where Matthew questioned Janine about her courses and they fell into an enthusiastic discussion of Plato. Matthew interrupted to draw their attention to a swirl of white-winged birds above a pan of water.

"But after all . . . . it's the artist in him that we really value, don't you agree? And what an artist he can be when he chooses to . . . oh, what an artist! I'm sure that if Plato were here with us now, he wouldn't quibble with the reality of *that*. It isn't the Idea of Flight, only a particular instance, but it's real enough to any poet. Plato included. Oh, yes, my dear friends, I'd bet my head on that!" He was talking with a kind of tender solicitude for the two of them, as though he were eager to overwhelm them with the best he had to give. He stood up and paced, flashing his glance between Felix's face and Janine's. "Do you know which is the greatest gift of all to cultivate?" he challenged, beaming, yet with an intensity that fixed the moment and its thought in their memories for use as a touchstone. "Shall I tell you? The child's eye, that's the great art. Seeing things as though for the first time. Perceiving everything, always, as though it were brand new in the world. As though you had never seen it before."

He gestured as if he were handing them one of the keys of his particular powers, for their own use, one of the precious keys of awareness. And they did bear his words away as his one explicit lesson to the two of them. But Felix was to wonder, much later on, whether that could have been Matthew's intention, aware as he was that they were all too young and raw. In any case, it was a redundant lesson to two who were just then tipsy with the silly sense that what they found in each other and gave was new, unique, not only for themselves, for all the world.

That afternoon he shared Janine's full response to his friend's sensitivity and wisdom, and was sure Matthew must be impressed by her understanding and charm, so their encounter was affording him a kind of proprietorial pride. The easy assurance of Matthew's gay paternal pat on Janine's trousered thigh, as he responded to her thanks at the end of the outing, stirred Felix's envy, but pleased him as the seal of Matthew's acceptance.

They were both silent at first during the drive to Felix's house. "She's a very attractive girl," Matthew said finally, flashing Felix a good-natured grin. "Oh, yes, one has to say that for her."

The afternoon had left Felix joyfully distrait. He nodded and merely murmured, "Oh, I know . . ."

"Will you tell me something, Felix?" Matthew spoke with his eyes fixed on the road. "Is it on account of her physical attractions that you're involved with her?"

"No," Felix objected. "No. We're friends, as I told you. We like each other . . . Well, how can I say . . .? I may be like a fly at a jampot. Of course there is that, but I think I can control it if I have to. She means other things to me as well . . ."

"Oh, yes, of course she does . . ." Matthew laughed banteringly. "But seriously, Felix, my friend, I think you must beware of hurting yourself over her."

"How can I hurt myself?" Felix almost shouted. "We make each other happy as friends. If there's a risk I'll just have to take it. What ought I to do? I can't refuse whatever life offers me for the sake of safety."

"Well, I think we'd better change the subject," Matthew said, still smiling affectionately. "You're obviously worked up about it. That's quite understandable."

One of Matthew's special favours to Felix was the occasional visit to Mary Fotheringham, and it was at her home, and by Matthew, that the subject of Janine was again raised between them. Felix's friend was very pleasant to look at, he told Mary,

". . . but I don't understand how any parent can saddle a child with a name like Janine."

"Why?" Felix asked.

"It's so vulgar, so would-be exotic. Don't you agree, Mary?"

"Janine?   It's pretentious," Mary shuddered. "Poor thing . . ."

"I never knew Janine was an exotic name," Felix said, "But anyway, if it is exotic and vulgar, what's the difference?" It was all he dared to say, but they could see his indignation. The subject was dropped.

But Matthew raised the subject of Janine some weeks later when Felix saw him in the bookshop. There was a play on at the Library Theatre that seemed worth seeing. Matthew wished Felix and Janine to be his guests. Felix was pleased on several counts. The invitation to Janine seemed to signal a sort of concession and truce.

The evening came. Janine picked Felix up in Lalapanzi, and they met Matthew and his partner — one of the girls who shared Janine's flat — at the theatre.   Felix found the first act absorbing enough, but at the end of it Matthew declared the production abominable and insisted on leaving. The girls acquiesced, and Felix was overruled.

They went to complete the evening at the home of Matthew's married sister where he was living as caretaker while the family was away on a holiday. It was an airy new mansion, but the furniture, paintings, and carpets did away with any hint of rawness. Felix sank into a deep floral upholstered armchair, expecting that the time would be passed with records and conversation. But very soon Matthew and his friend Monica grew boisterous, laughed, chased each other like excited lovers, and disappeared from the sitting room.

Felix's thoughts played a moment over the notion, the hint hanging like a fruit among the leaves of the situation, that Janine and he were also lovers. Oddly, it was almost as though they had never before been alone together. All the same, he did no more than smile his affection at her. Matthew and Monica might reappear at any moment. It was Janine who seemed determined to take advantage of their absence. She came and sat on the carpet before his armchair and looked earnestly into his face. "Felix," she said, staring as though she wished to stare away the smile from his face.

"Janine," he responded, his smile persisting.

She lowered her eyes. "I've got to tell you something."

"Well, tell!"

"A whole lot of things, in fact, about myself. There's so much I've never told you . . ."

"Don't I just know that! But it's only the way things have happened. I'm going to find it all out in time, aren't I?"

"I must explain it all now . . ."

"Now? All? Well, fine. I'd love to know everything, Janine, all about you."

"You see, Felix," she began, with a pleading look and an intimate solemnity that thrilled him. "It's my parents. Do you know what rich Jewish parents are like?" He shrugged, and she looked downward and traced a pattern in the carpet with her finger.

"They hold on, to everything and everyone. Especially daughters. Mine are strong. My father made
all his own money, a lot, I never told you . . . And
he's proud and he likes the feeling of power. I
suppose he needs it, because, I think, somewhere
inside, underneath, he's really weak and frightened. My mother's different, but she's also demanding and hysterical. They give me everything they
think I could wish for, even though they don't
understand me. And they expect me to fit in with
a certain pattern. I can't, of course. It isn't my
way of life. But at the same time, they've got so
much power over me, emotionally and so on. I
can't hurt them . . ."

As she continued Felix grew bewildered. She
had talked to him often about her feelings and
ideas concerning books and art, truth, morality
and relationships, but never about her circumstances. Circumstances had seemed to both of
them irrelevant. What she was saying now was in a
sense more personal than anything she had ever
told him before — yet the case she was presenting
was conventional and 'realistic', and scored across
the individual, the Janine he knew. Strange as it
all was, he felt privileged at being allowed to hear
it, pleased that he was being asked to understand
and sympathise with her in the most practical prob-
lems of her life. This was an unexpected step on
the way of their growing together, and she seemed
to have chosen to make the step in this well-ap-
pointed room so that the atmosphere of the place
would help him understand the background out
of which her difficulties arose.

"They even know what kind of person they'd like me to marry," she was going on. "And if I wanted someone different, they would put everything in my way. I would have to fight. There would be a terrible, destructive, absolute war between them and me . . ."

She broke off. A spider was moving, in short runs, up the cream panel of a door. She drew off one of her shoes, rose and approached. Felix gathered himself to protest. But he had been so eager, while she was speaking, to follow and feel with her that now, when it came to checking her next move, he faltered. Her immediate decision, and then the neat brisk thrust with which she killed the spider, seemed a trained precaution, a hygienic habit absorbed from the immaculate background she'd been describing to him, and her assured unsentimental act seemed the final stroke of the description. When she resumed speaking, he released the breath he had been holding and continued to listen as though there had been no interruption.

"I know that you feel a lot for me, Felix. And you know I feel for you. And . . . you're probably hoping for . . . things, expecting certain things. Things you need. But, this is what I have to tell you, because of everything, I can't get involved . . ." He shook his head, more than ever bewildered, as her message at last emerged: it had, after all, more to do with himself than with her. "That is why, you understand, we can't see each other any more . . ."

He cried out, "What? Why? Why? No, I don't understand. What makes that necessary? I've never asked . . . I've never . . . I've never said anything to you . . . made . . . demands . . ." She had no cause, no scope for a rebuff. He'd never *made* love to her. But he was stopped from protesting with all the urgency he felt, by the sense that to express his grief would be now to make love and give her reason to retreat from him. "It isn't necessary," was all he could argue. "What have I done? *Why* should we suddenly have to stop being friends? *Friends?* Why?"

Anguished as he was, his words were insufficient to move her. "It's better that it should be now. Please understand and try to accept. You know I'm sorry to lose your friendship, but if we leave it to later it will be worse, it will do more damage."

"If you're sorry, then why lose it? Why've you got to lose it?" But to all his further arguments and pleas she only sadly shook her head, and at last, recognising she was adamant, he sank into himself, frozen, terrified, and unable to understand how, when, why he had lost her. He turned his eyes away from her face with its acid new meaning. And for some moments they sat in silence. Then, as though frightened, she moved, trying to catch his eye again.

"Felix . . . please, Felix . . ."

Matthew and Monica entered the room on the final bounce of their gambol round the garden or bedrooms or wherever it had been. Felix sat in his stunned state and the three others moved and murmured remotely around him like surgeon and nurses round a half-anesthetized patient. Something was being done about tea. Then Janine and

Matthew were in the kitchen in subdued, agitated conversation. Nervously, Janine was sending a noisy gush of water again and again from the tap into the sink. All at once, the girls were leaving, the two together in Janine's car. Then they were gone, and Matthew was explaining that Janine had told him what had happened between them. He was very sorry. He hoped Felix wasn't going to take it too much to heart. He oughtn't to go home tonight but would do better to remain there with him. Felix was indifferent, acquiescent. Matthew guarded and comforted him that night, gently, circumspectly, as though he'd been grossly bereaved or were in danger of suicide.

Janine had, in fact, dealt him a bit of death. There was another, and another, on the following days at university. He glimpsed her across this vestibule, down that corridor, beyond that lawn, unchanged in her looks, in her manner toward anyone, but turning away from the sight of him, where before she would have run to meet him.

But after a week he was reprieved, resurrected. Seeing him in the foyer of Central Block, she turned toward and not away from him, smiled shyly and fondly, and came near. "Felix . . . Felix . . ." she said, into his still frozen face, "People have been telling me, I can see how you've been feeling. I'm sorry. Let's be friends again."

"But you . . . Janine . . . What you . . ."

"It was a mistake. Don't ask me to explain. I'm sorry. I'm sorry. We must just forget everything I said . . . Oh, Felix, I've been missing you so much."

There was no choice, no ground of hesitation for

him. Breath and colour rushed to his face, he laughed and stammered, "Let's . . . let's go and sit down somewhere. O gosh! Oh, God . . ."

"Come to Lalapanzi," she said, and it was there that he asked, "But Janine, Janine, why? What was it all about? How did I frighten you?"

"It wasn't that," she protested. "Oh Felix, I made a promise not to tell you, but I must. It was Matthew. He wanted to help you."

Felix's scalp began to tingle. "What do you mean?"

"He came to the flat twice, to talk to me about you."

He exclaimed irrelevantly, "That's how he knew Monica!"

Janine nodded. "He said he was very concerned about you. Said he's known you so much longer than I have and knows what your needs are. He asked me if I was prepared to go . . . to give certain things to you. Oh, Felix, I just hadn't thought about that kind of thing. Otherwise I would damage you."

"But you knew you couldn't damage me!"

"While he was talking to me I didn't know anything. I didn't even know how to leave you. He worked it out . . . what I should say to you."

"There was something so unreal about it all, about everything you did that evening." Felix stared hard at her and she looked unhappily away.

"Matthew! Matthew! Matthew!" he groaned, drumming with his fist on the seat of the car. "Damn him! Oh, damn him, and his special arrangements!"

"Ah Felix! That's not like you," Janine said. "He really meant the best for you. And anyway, we're together again. He's made no difference to us."

"Yes, that's true," said Felix, unable yet to risk anything, "I suppose."

He stared fixedly at her face, trying to recall what it had seemed to him eight days before.

Knowledge

When Felix wrote a story about a bridge-builder that showed he knew nothing about the building of bridges, Mr de Waal said, "No! Look . . . look . . . You've never built a bridge, have you? If you want to write a story about something you don't know from your own experience, you must find out about it. You must look it up. Otherwise it will lack authenticity. Look, haven't you got an encyclopaedia?"

"Not really," said Felix. "Actually only an old set that's incomplete."

Mr de Waal wanted to see the set. It began at AND to AUS. The volume between BIS to CAL and DEM to EDW was missing, along with the next but one, just before EVA to FRA and five others.

"There's plenty for you to find out about in all these volumes." Mr de Waal smiled. "Even though they're old — hey? — you'll be quite well-informed if all you read is this part that isn't lost."

"Twenty-two volumes," Felix said.

"Yes. Only twenty-two volumes. I think they should keep you busy for a little while." Mr de Waal laughed out loud and Felix joined in.

"Yes. Pile them up over your desk and use them. Read about bridges and boats and China and magic and painting. Look up whatever you want to write about — make sure you know about whatever you're referring to."

Wanting to understand, to get things right, to please, Felix asked, "But what if the volume I want is missing?"

Mr de Waal smiled, shrugged, flicked his hands apart like a spread of wings, turning the problem free. "You can't know everything . . ."

So that was how Edwin Shaver's twenty-two volumes came to be stacked on Felix's desk, where his eyes rested on them as he pondered while writing, and the legends on the spines became embedded in his memory: ITA to KYS, MUN to ODD, ODE to PAY, VET to ZYM . . .

Felix and Edwin had first become friendly, like a pair of disciples, through their interest in what Skipper Ross had to teach. Once Skipper had gone from The Home there was no one to share it with but each other, and that also went for their interest in education and other vaguer ambitions. Felix now admired the self-assurance he had resented when Edwin was a new boy. He found his elevated style of speech half-ludicrous and half-enviable, but he was altogether impressed by Edwin's determined ambitiousness.

Like Felix, Edwin was a spastic, though his pattern was different — his speech was easier and he could trot at almost a running pace and make his way without help in the swimming pool as long as he could hold onto the side. He seemed to have a way of using the need to control the rigidities and spasms of his body, making something purposeful and implacable out of involuntary jerkiness and slowness. He moved like a lordly machine. His left arm would swing outward in a reflex stiffening in moments of stress, but he turned it into a commanding gesture. When his limbs pushed him into a stumble or other mishap, he righted himself immediately, adjusting his glasses with a fierce stab of his forefinger to the bridge of his nose, while the tremble of his drawn-up chin and taut mouth expressed only indignation.

"My ambition," Edwin announced during break at school one day when he and Felix and one or two others had chosen to stay in the classroom, "is to know everything there is to know. Because knowledge, my boys, is power." He was perched on top of his desk, the way he always sat when he had to write without his typewriter, practising his signature on the back of an exercise book: E. Shaver, E. P. J. Shaver, Edwin Peter Jarrold Shaver, Edwin P. Shaver, E. Shaver, Esq . . . With his left arm held rigid, he was anchoring the exercise book alongside his leg while, with the fingers of his right hand knotted around the pencil, he designed signature after signature, trying to make each one show as little as possible of his tremor.

He continued, with one of his diplomatic little dips into slang, "And I'm willing to bet any of you guys anything you like that it can be done."

"Hundred pounds," one of the others chipped

in.

"A million pounds to one pound!" Edwin went on, absorbing cynical giggles with a serene nod of his head. "That's what I'm prepared to bet that it can be accomplished. All it requires is determination . . ." — he wrote "DETERMINATION!" in the midst of his signatures — "application and persistence, provided one possesses the ability to assimilate data and, of course, to understand intelligently whatever one memorizes. That — poof, poof! — that ought to go without saying, actually."

"What is data?" Felix asked.

"What? Oh! Haw haw haw! Good joke, good joke!" Edwin bellowed, miming a pat on Felix's head. "What is data, indeed!"

"But I want to know," said Felix.

"Do my ears deceive me, dear boy? You really don't know? Such ignorance, tut, tut! Well then, I'll tell you with the greatest of pleasure. Data is the plural of datum. Hm . . .?" He paused, long enough for Felix to begin, "But . . .", then continued, "And a datum is definable as a relevant fact. 'Relevant' is the operative term, you understand? Therefore, data equals relevant or apposite facts, or indeed — let me rather say and/or — figures in any field of study. There you are! Elementary! Q.E.D.! And you ought, speaking grammatically, to have asked, 'What *are* data?' Hm . . .?"

By this time Felix couldn't remember what had been said about data in the first place. But he had been learning many things from Edwin, who was two years his senior though they were in the same class at school. (Edwin had hinted that he had

had to fight his way through neglect, illness and even cruelty in earlier years, but preferred talking about the future.) Those two extra years seemed to have equipped him not only with more learning than Felix possessed but with other kinds of knowledge and strength that Felix felt he never would possess.

The *Britannica* was Edwin's, one of the unusual possessions he had brought with him when he first came to The Home. His portable typewriter was another. He had a watch and there were some other books and two boxes of what he called "my therapeutic equipment and personal effects". It was all far too much to fit into a bedside locker, and he was allowed to keep it in a cupboard in the supervisor's office — perhaps because he was an orphan and The Home was his only home. In any case, all the particular things about him — the possessions, the cupboard, the many letters he wrote and received, the judge who visited him three or four times a year, his quick expertness in the Scouts with Morse and the theory of first aid and knots and staves, his way of speaking, and all the information he was able to give when showing visitors around the boys' section — all that made him seem more important than just another inmate.

Another thing was money — not so much money he had as money he needed and somehow found. To Felix a shilling or two seemed a lot, but Edwin spoke of, obtained and spent as much as several pounds at a time. It was once when he needed money that he offered the incomplete 1910

Encyclopaedia Britannica to Felix for two guineas. "You must appreciate that it is printed on India paper and bound in calf leather, dear boy. I'm sure that I could get more for it, considerably more, if I made further enquiries. But with your interests I am confident that you would make excellent use of it." Grumbling at the age and incompleteness of the set, Dad reluctantly agreed to buy it and Felix felt as he handed the money over that he had done his friend a favour.

The tall, neat volumes with their scuffed gilt-lettered spines were loaded on the back seat of Dad's car one Sunday and taken home. Now and then, during the next few school holidays, Felix pulled a volume out to browse through it, or to read about Chess or Hypnotism or Mind (he was looking for Mind Over Matter) or to stare at the nude female figures that illustrated Sculpture. Dad occasionally looked up something like Palestine or Potato or Money, but if the wanted volume was missing he said, "What's the use if it's incomplete!" When the war ended, Felix wrote to the publishers to find out what it would cost to complete the set. The quotation was two guineas per volume, so he gave up the idea and somehow never told Edwin about his enquiry. The set was stored in a low cupboard with a door which tended to swing ajar. One day the cat sharpened her claws on the spines, scratching away more of the finish on several of them and rawly ploughing up the soft leather on BIS to CAL, REF to SAI and SAI to SHU.

After Felix left The Home, Edwin stayed on and soon after was appointed assistant to the supervisor of the boys. It was the first time an inmate had become a member of staff. Mainly to see him, Felix would visit The Home from time to time. Edwin accepted occasional invitations to visit Felix for a few hours of talk and chess and a meal.

Felix had been accepted at a private college in town where he could finish his schooling. He was surprised one day nearly two months after starting, to find Edwin in the classroom. Edwin attended regularly after that, though it was never explained what arrangements had been made for paying the college fees or for permission from the matron of The Home to take the necessary hours off every day. All Edwin cared to say about it was, "One has to matriculate, dear boy, which evidently is something you well understand. Matriculation is a necessary, or let me rather say unavoidable hurdle if one intends taking a university degree. I intend taking, initially, the Bachelor of Arts degree, the B.A., and after that, Honours and an L.L.B. or a Master's, and ultimately a D. Phil., that is to say a Doctorate of Philosophy. Quite. Quite. Hm . . .?" He signed his name: E. Shaver, B.A. (Hons.), L.L.B., M.A., D. Phil.

For the time being, Felix could not look forward with anything like the same composure. He was still recovering after the steep step up from the commercial Standard Eight he had passed at the Home school to the academic matriculation level of the classes at the college. The aloofness or shyness that isolated him from his fellow students was not all that made him feel out of place at first. He had joined the English class a few days late and found himself plunged into the roisterous obscurities of a play the teacher called *Henry IV*, and discovered after several more lessons that it was by Shakespeare. As for poetry, he was surprised to be told he was right when he guessed that "Intimations of Immortality" was about a baby growing up.

But it was his rawness that allowed him a virgin excitement when he was introduced to Keats. "The Eve of St Agnes" and "Ode to a Nightingale" made him realize for the first time how much more there was to poetry than the rhyme and metre he had been triumphant over in his own verses, written about one a month since Standard Five or Six. He begged a neglected volume of Keats from a cousin's bookshelf and read for his own pleasure, and when he wrote yearned toward the same poignant sweetness. The power of poetry became a mystery he longed to understand.

A hint that there were those who, for all their familiarity with poetry, still felt this mystery urgently for themselves, came one day when an English lesson was given by a new teacher, a man with an apprehensive manner and a soft hesitant way of speech. With rather pleading, defensive gestures, he set about explaining not facts about the set-work but feelings about poetry itself, which, with reverence, he pronounced "poyetry". Everything about him invited derision from the raucous class, which it expressed with mocking inattentiveness. Habitually respectful of teachers and even more of newcomers, Felix was ashamed of this rudeness. But despite his curiosity about what the man might have to tell, he found his presentation unengaging. Not surprisingly, he gave no more than that one lesson. But his manner had been unusual enough to leave a little legend and a nickname, Old Poytry.

Later Felix thought he saw him on several occasions coming or going in the vicinity of the college. At least he saw a man who usually walked with the Afrikaans teacher, her husband presumably — a man who moved in a way that combined shyness and jauntiness, carried a folded magazine tucked under one arm, and always wore a hat tipped rakishly to one side but with the brim drawn down as though to shelter his eyes. Because of the hat Felix could not be certain that he was Old Poytry.

To Edwin, attendance at the college meant that he had to make his way between The Home and town by tram and by foot. As the months passed and the examinations grew closer, the number of extra classes for revision was increased and sometimes lectures ended late in the afternoon. Climbing the path up the koppie toward The Home one evening after dusk, he was set upon by a prowler who pushed him down, breaking his glasses, and robbed him of his watch and money. After two days, he returned to college with grazes on his hand and temple and explained, "If the scoundrel had not sprung on me from behind I might have got my special grip on his neck and overpowered him by applying pressure on certain neural paths. There is a way of producing complete immobilization. Nothing to it if you know the technique, nothing to it at all . . ."

But the attack had left him pale and over-tense, and not long after, his college attendance was threatened because he began to suffer from a fear of crossing streets. The trouble was brought under control through a course of treatments by the college principal, Mr Franklin, who held an American degree in psychology and was an expert hypnotist, and Edwin was able to continue at college and to sit the examinations.

He and Felix, permitted extra time and the use of typewriters, were given a room apart to write in. When the results showed that both of them had failed in the same two subjects, which did not match their picture of their respective strengths, it was natural to wonder if some of their answer papers had not gone astray. Nevertheless, Edwin arranged to sit again at the earliest opportunity, and passed.

Felix had not learned his results for several days because Dad and Moh at first contrived to keep the news of his failure from him. His outrage when he discovered their ploy blurred his disappointment in the result itself. "How dare you keep the truth away from me," he shouted, "the truth about myself! I'll die if I have to be ashamed of my own truth and hide away from it. I have to know . . ."

Despite his anger they resisted his wish to push on as Edwin was doing, insisting that the papers must have been lost and that it would be wrong if he had to go through the ordeal of writing again. The re-mark Mr Franklin applied for brought no change in the result, and it looked as though Felix was in a cul de sac as far as his education was concerned. Mr Franklin showed the way out. He knew of Felix's ambition, and told Mr Greenspan he could recommend as a suitable "creative writing coach", Mr Johan de Waal who was the literary editor of *The Monthly Review*.

It was Old Poytry Felix found in the principal's office on the day he went there to meet his coach. Mr Franklin was not present to introduce them and they waited a few moments in uncertainty. Then the man said, "Are . . . you . . . Felix?" thrusting each word out with deliberation as though to propel it across the barrier of his hesitancy, but reminding Felix of the pace of some of his solemn pronouncements and quotations in his lecture of months ago. Their identities confessed, Mr de Waal suggested that they make their way to his office for the first lesson. But after walking a few yards in the street he decided that the journey of several blocks would be too much for Felix. So the lesson took place in a café near the college. One of the two people at a nearby table was the college art teacher. Mr de Waal greeted the couple heartily and with a kind of flourish made a one-sided introduction: "This is Felix. He's going to be a marvellous writer."

It was, of course, a joke, gently satirising Felix's aspirations. At the same time, it was acknowl-

edgement and even encouragement of those aspirations. Felix became flushed with excitement.
Mr de Waal had been given a handful of Felix's
writings by Mr Franklin, and as he now commented
on these, Felix began to realise that he had
infinities to learn. But there was a phrase here
and there that pleased Mr de Waal, and it was
his way of acknowledging this pleasure that intoxi-
cated Felix. Each successful touch was hailed with
extraordinary signs of excitement and with laughter. Felix sniggered helplessly with pride and
pleasure at being praised and celebrated in this
overwhelming way. It was difficult to identify the
present Mr de Waal with the teacher who had
been paralyzed with awkwardness in the face of
that classroom of impatient boys and girls, difficult to know how such a person could have seemed unengaging.

As Felix grew familiar with him over the following months, it was Mr de Waal's laughter that came
to seem perhaps the most extraordinary thing
about him. Though hearty and free it somehow
carried all sorts of serious implications. Like a
bolt of lightning or a ceremony, it illuminated
and altered what it touched. But even without
laughter Mr de Waal produced an aura which
intensified the moment. His eyes had something
to do with it, the eyes he so often hid along with
the breadth of his brow under the wild tilt of his
hat. They were vividly blue, under tangled sandy
eyebrows which contributed to their expressive-
ness. When they weren't flashing excitement,
awe, apprehension or moments of secretly expli-

cable terror, they were beaming tenderly shrewd amusement that could take off wildly into hilarity or deepen to a look that cherished whatever or whomever it was resting on. And his hands also played their part, dancing with the meaning, shaping and reshaping it, as he spoke.

A secret history — his broad shoulders, lopsidedly hunching a little toward his vulnerable neck, carried the weight of it — predisposed him to receive each word or situation or piece of writing with a warmth that magnified its significance, or to shrink as though it implied a blow, an affront. He shrank, for example, as he returned Matthew Kahn's little book to Felix who had brought it to him as a discovery: "No, look . . . When I'd finished reading it I threw it across the room. You see, if there wasn't a whole school—hey?—a whole university of followers of T.S. Eliot, then one might find some time for this stuff—one might suspect that there is something real in it." And Eliot was no favourite of Mr de Waal's, as Felix knew. It never became possible for him to predict with certainty whether an expansive or a negative response would be forthcoming. The clues were guarded by a personal reticence: polite curiosity about himself was one identifiable thing Mr de Waal would shrink from.

Yet there was something lavish in the way he shared his excitements. "Look . . . Look . . . Listen to this!" he urged one day as soon as he had sat down with Felix. The knuckles of one hand came up in front of his smiling lips, while the other fist pummelled his thigh like a gavel. "Yes. Yes. Yes.

Yes . . ." he almost hissed, and it seemed that his thought was still unfolding in his imagination. "Look . . . If a farmer goes to a scientist, he can say: 'I have this piece of land. Now, if I sow this quantity of seed, and if I put in this quantity of such-and-such fertilizer, and I give the field so-and-so much irrigation, how many bags of mielies per morgen will I reap?' And the scientist will be able to tell him: 'Under those circumstances you can expect to reap so many bags per morgen.' But if the farmer goes to God — hey? — and tells God about his land and his seed and his fertilizer and his water, and asks God, 'How many bags of mielies per morgen will I reap?' — God will say, 'I don't know. But, go ahead. Try it. You'll get a *lot*.'"

Mr de Waal's creed, for which the college English class had lacked patience, concerned not poetry alone but all of literature, the writing of which was not separable from responsive reading, and the whole of which, with the other arts, was tied up with life. "Art and life and God are one," he affirmed. Felix had never guessed art could be taken so seriously, or life so religiously, or God so earthily. Imperative behind all art there were "the eternal verities", there were venerable traditions and secrets of art, and yet all was essentially known only in the heart, so everything was thrown back on the artist's self, the flux of his feelings rather than the predictabilities of the mind, his own experienceof life, his individual style.

Groping to understand how he was to achieve his style, his personal voice, his known subject matter,

Felix once asked, "Should I write about my own life?"

Mr de Waal pressed his knuckles nervously against his mouth. "No . . . Look . . . If you mean your physical disability, that isn't going to allow you your imaginative detachment, not so? It sets you the trap of self-pity, and other traps nearly as bad. But—hey?— in any case, it's too obvious— yes? yes?— too easy to be of any artistic significance." In this form, Felix saw, art was going to require on his own part, too, a certain reticence.

The lessons were interrupted after a few months by Felix's last and longest stay on the farm with Skipper Ross. One day he repeated some of Mr de Waal's comments on Dickens to Skipper: "His approach is sentimental and didactic, so he makes a lot of his characters either all good or all bad, instead of mixed, like real people."

"But you have to have a clear picture of what is good if you're going to give an illustration that explains truth," Skipper answered. "The only books that are worthwhile are those that can teach us lessons about goodness. The rest are only distractions that prevent people from seeking the truth."

Felix said nothing. What Skipper was saying was in keeping with what he had been teaching all along, but now Felix knew that as far as literature was concerned, as he was trying to learn about it from Mr de Waal, there was something wrong with Skipper's argument. He tried to forget about it, but an uncomfortable feeling of being at odds recurred from time to time for a moment as long as he remained on the farm. His stay ended when he finally discovered that he could not live up to Skipper's expectations. Something prevented him from ever telling Edwin about his failure, and although once he'd left the farm he never visited or wrote to Skipper again, Skipper's ideas were, in a way, kept alive for him by Edwin.

Mr de Waal did not drive but came by tram to the Greenspan's house to give Felix his twice weekly lessons. One day not long after they were resumed, he arrived while Felix was eating a belated lunch. In the place of the food he had to leave, Felix took a handful of almonds which, one by one, he pushed into his mouth and munched as the lesson got under way. Mr de Waal was talking about a book called *Masters of English Literature* which he had brought for Felix to read.

"You can leave out the chapters on the Age of Reason," he was saying. "The spirit of poetry has got nothing to do with logic and reason. . ." Then, as Felix put the fourth nut to his lips, he broke off and said sharply, "No . . . No, look! Throw that away! Hey?"

Shocked, Felix silently emptied his hand into the wastepaper basket. For a few minutes harsh resentment deafened him to the progress of the lesson. How dared the man so rudely vent his irritation on him! Who was he, anyway? The teacher who received a few pounds a months from Dad for these lessons . . . A magazine journalist whose own bits of writing lacked the polish and dignity of real literature . . .

This anger could not survive Mr de Waal's celebratory warmth as the lesson went on, and as it receded Felix began to see that his tutor's snappishness was not a nervous response to the ungainliness of his movements as he nibbled the nuts, but was a demand for due respect to the subject they were engaged with. It was not much after this day that his judgement of Mr de Waal as a writer also began to alter. Reading more of the stories and essays that appeared in *The Monthly Review*, he grew gradually to appreciate that they were more than the rough, light pieces they had at first seemed because of their colloquial style and open humour, that they were brilliantly original and magical. He began to understand that, however thrillingly he was being inducted into his apprenticeship as writer, Mr de Waal was only incidentally his teacher, out of the same brute necessity that made him work on *The Monthly Review* and other publications as subeditor, proofreader and seller of advertising space: he was primarily an author in his own right, one of rare attractiveness and power.

The rules of his thinking were less easy to define than Skipper Ross's, and Felix tottered precariously as he strained to share a viewpoint in which the moment's feeling, or humour, or art could always give an unpredictable shape to the truth. In time he realised that in fact there were no rules. Paradox could be just as false as banality. The important thing was to be open to experience, to recognize the fascination of human life together with all its imperfections, of people, without wanting to improve them, and to follow one's heart.

Mr de Waal's way, into the marvels of art, was as much of a flight as Skipper's way had been, yet it was also a return to the human earth. When, among the columns of a story Mr de Waal was showing him in a magazine, Felix noticed a cartoon depicting a tight-rope walker performing without a rope, captioned "Mind over matter," he said, "That's something I believe in. Anyone can really do that if they use the powers of the mind."

"Oh, yes . . . ?" said Mr de Waal, glancing at the cartoon. He looked uneasy and was seized by a fit of coughing. When it stopped he put one hand on Felix's shoulder and with the other slapped his own leg. "No, look . . ." he said eagerly. "It's enough when there is a rope. Hey?" A loud laugh burst out of him and he thumped his thigh. "Even when there is a rope and a net underneath, it's enough. Because . . . Look!" He broke off, laughing wildly, pressing his knuckles to his mouth as though to quell his mirth. "It's enough, because — hey? hey? — when there is a rope, you can fall off."

Felix laughed to applaud the joke and let the subject go. He felt a little disconcerted but knew it was no use trying to insist or explain the belief to Mr de Waal. Arguments were not his way of dealing: he would either turn them into jokes or shrink from the arguer in a way that seemed almost frightened. But soon there was a different feeling, a kind of relief at the dismissal of Mind Over Matter. There could be an end of uneasy feelings about seeing the powers and attractions of matter. And there was more to it than indul-

gence: matter had its own ways of being important for writing. Apart from inspirations and fantasies and jokes, there were facts, techniques and
disciplines that had to be given their due. Mr de
Waal told Felix to take a daily walk and pay attention to his surroundings, to avoid the danger of
becoming absorbed in introspection. And he insisted on a solid background of knowledge to
whatever one chose to write about. If a writer
had an inspiration, that was manna, but he must
always remain humble enough to check the vali-
dity of what came into his head by the facts of
his own experience or else by the dictionary, the
encyclopaedia or other authoritative sources.
This was the insistence that led to the rescue of
Edwin's *Britannica* from its obscure cupboard, to
be stood closest to Felix when he was at work.

Edwin was one of the people to whom Felix
tried to convey an idea of Mr de Waal's unique-
ness. "Just to show you how he looks at things,"
he explained on one of the now infrequent occasions when they saw each other, "he told me the
other day about meeting an artist friend of his
who said something he liked very much. He told
Mr de Waal he had had an exhibition which had
been very successful. When Mr de Waal asked
him if he had sold many paintings, he answered,
'No, not one. But . . . one man *spat*.'"

"But dear boy," Edwin protested, "why should
anyone regard such a rude gesture as a sign of
success?"

"Well, it proved that he hadn't painted so as to
please people, but so as to move them."

"Evidently it proved that," Edwin argued on, "but as a consequence of not pleasing his public, he sold none of his paintings."

Felix shook his head urgently. "That's not what matters. What matters is art for art's sake."

"Art for art's sake? What does that imply?"

"Well, it's creating because you believe in it, not just for money or fame."

"In an idealistic way, hm? I see. Well, that's quite commendable."

"But at the same time the artist must be humble. Mr de Waal says he must approach everything, other artists, his own work, the whole of life, in a spirit of humility—otherwise his creativity will go sour."

"Well, I daresay a modicum of humility would serve as an appropriate safeguard for most sorts of people," said Edwin, losing interest. And Felix realized that he had chosen an inappropriate line.

In the city reference library, where he went to read some of Mr de Waal's earlier work, Felix was moved to discover that humility could not always have been an article of his credo. There had been a stage when his poems and essays contained wild assumptions and proclamations about the superiority of his calling and his standing among men. What moved Felix was the certainty that pain, if not calamity, must have intervened to displace that romantic arrogance, and the thought that it might easily have been replaced by bitterness instead of the graciousness and warmth that had come.

So these qualities seemed even more precious than before and a dimension was added for Felix when, for example, Mr de Waal one afternoon brought a large bouquet of red roses for Moh. The romance of such a gesture was incongruous in terms of Moh's life, but the writer saw things in the light of a different world and cared to claim her from the drabness of hers for a moment.

Again, when Mr and Mrs de Waal visited the Greenspans of an evening, Dad expanded and glowed in the warmth of a delighted audience for his prodigiously rambling anecdotes about his earlier days. No one else, no one in the family at any rate, had ever had much patience for them. Whatever enrichment and order Mr de Waal's imagination was bringing to the stories, Felix also had to credit him with generosity and gentleness.

After about eighteen months Mr de Waal declared that he had nothing more to teach Felix. Was it one of his jokes? Dad wanted a visible sign of Felix's training and at first pressed Mr de Waal into continuing the lessons. But a few weeks later there was a visible sign, when the *Monthly Review* accepted a story of Felix's for publication. Moreover, a publisher had engaged Mr de Waal for a project which required him to move to Cape Town.

The regular formal lessons ended, but Felix's tutelage continued unchanged in his own mind. He wrote to Mr de Waal and sent him his next completed story, and received a reply that sustained him. In fact Felix now needed Mr de Waal's acknowledgement more than he needed his guidance. He could not regard the new piece of writing as real until Mr de Waal had read it, as though till then the type might have vanished from the paper. So it was a happy thing for him when the Cape Town project failed and the de Waals returned to Johannesburg after a few months. Once again he could see his mentor from time to time, and these encounters—whether Felix took his newest story to Mr de Waal at his new place of work, or whether the de Waals paid a friendly visit to the Greenspans' house—were always important occasions for Felix.

His excitement partly came from a kind of acceptance, which after all he was even less used to for himself than for his father. This was something he found also in the de Waal's circle, at the occasional parties they invited him to— twice when a new book of Mr de Waal's was published. In other company, even in wider family gatherings, Felix often sat silent after bidding in vain for a hearing or making a remark that generated only a flat response, himself bored by the conversation and unable to think of anything to say that might command attention. But at the de Waal's parties, where many of the guests were writers, artists, actors or publishers and the conversation—given its center and level by the host —dazzled Felix with its brilliance and fun, he found himself listened and responded to; they even laughed at his jokes.

But there was more to it than congenial acceptance. It was as though, when he was in Mr de Waal's presence, sharing through propinquity in his fantastical enriching vision of whatever came into view or into mind, accepted by him as a novice of the creative brotherhood, Felix was endowed with wings with which to soar above whatever made existence mundane, solemn, dull, ordinary.

"Oh, Lord, Felix! I think you're so brave to go into all that," Mrs de Waal exclaimed when Felix came to her husband's office with the news that he was accepted as a student at the university.

"My God! Think of all that still to go through!" Mr de Waal took the idea up. "And then, afterwards . . . Hey?"

"Afterwards! Oooh . . ." Mrs de Waal moaned and laughed simultaneously over a preposterous memory. "The confusion! I was never so confused in my life. Do you remember what it was like, Johan?"

"Yes! Yes! We knew, once we had graduated, that we had been educated to a high level. But it took us a long time to discover — hey? — that it was a high level of . . . of . . ." He broke off, laughing.

His wife supplied, "Ignorance! Oooh . . .!"

"Yes! Yes! Or of — hey? — a high level of *silliness* . . ."

"And I," said Felix, only half mock-ruefully, "have got to study for three years before I get up to that level!"

"Ah, no, shame, Felix!" Mrs de Waal protested when the laughter subsided. "I was only remembering how confused I was."

In fact Mr de Waal had asserted long before that Felix could benefit as a writer from the experience of university and some academic background and had provided a testimonial to help gain him a matric exemption. By the time he entered university, Edwin had been taking university courses in psychology and economics by correspondence for some years. He and Felix had seen each other once or twice during this time and Edwin had talked about the lecturers and fellow students he had met through a summer school. There was a note of intensity, of pride and unburdening, in what he had to say of a girl student who had accepted him as her lover. "What is particularly beautiful and delightful to me is the way she wants me to bring her breasts into our love-play. She likes to have them stroked and squeezed and kissed and even gently nibbled. I knew, of course, that the breasts were erogenous zones, but she has taught me what an important role they can play in erotic contact."

Felix had never dreamed that a real girl could be like that, especially not a university student, yet here was Edwin with first-hand knowledge. "Edwin," he pleaded, "what did she . . .? I mean, how did you . . .?"

"How did I get her to love me, old boy, is that what you want to know?" Edwin flicked a finger and thumb, like signalling an easy command or turning a switch. "Just positive thinking, dear chap. Nothing to it, really, when you practise consistently. I always form a clear and vivid mental image of what I want, and then it's just a matter, so to speak, if you'll pardon the pun—haw haw!—of mind over matter."

Felix nodded as though it were explained, but the picture of the girl wanting those caresses was so fantastic that he did not know how to fit it into his reality, and when at later encounters Edwin did not refer to her again he did not know how to reopen the interesting subject.

When Uncle Lewis died, Mr de Waal cast a surprising light even on death. On the evening of that very day, the de Waals paid the Greenspans a visit which had been previously arranged. They received the news and gave their condolences ceremoniously enough, but after Dad went off to be with his widowed sister-in-law, Mr de Waal, who had once met Uncle Lewis but, as he had told Felix, had not cared for his cleverness or his way of showing it, became as fanciful and jocular as usual. "Why don't you have a drink as well?" he said to Felix as he accepted his own. "We could have a little wake — hey? It's the right time to get tipsy and tell stories of all the things you can remember about your uncle — especially the funny things. It's right that the best sort of parties, the most light-hearted sort — hey? — should happen when somebody dies."

For a moment, thinking of Dad's loss — his brother had been his hero — Felix felt chilled at this playfulness. Surely it was callous? But Mr de Waal was *his* hero and was being consistent with himself as well as acting out a piece of his own wisdom: the obvious was never to be trusted, and to have respected mournfulness and solemnity at such a time would have been to have acted obviously. The laughter was a means of dispelling the gloom in the house, but there was also a three-fold challenge in it: apart from the challenge to convention, Felix's imaginative agility and courage was being challenged, and death itself was being challenged.

Felix was disappointed with university from the first, because the choice of English set-works did not accord with Mr de Waal's canon. Later his dissatisfaction increased when he found the books being subjected to an unimpassioned analysis, as though they were codes of some sort, instead of living miraculous things as Mr de Waal had presented them to him. Besides, he was finding scarcely any time for writing. Early in his second year, when the process was beginning to be applied to *Humphrey Clinker* which he had read with particular pleasure on Mr de Waal's recommendation, he decided that he would stand no more of this solemn vandalism and gave up the university.

Dad, who believed that a degree behind an author's name would help to sell his books, was disappointed, but helped Felix mitigate his failure by creating a job for him in the office of his timber yard. Felix typed letters, filed invoices and absorbed the atmosphere of the fierce scramble for livelihood under the looming power station cooling towers. Something in it all, the cluttered sprawl of the yard, the noise of machines, traffic, work, voices, the variety of people who came into watching-and-listening distance of the cubicle where he worked, excited him, enlivened him with urgent inspirations of all sorts, which mostly had dissipated by the time he got home to his quiet room where he was free to write.

"No, look . . ." said Mr de Waal when Felix complained to him, "If the muse flirts with you in Newtown, you must be glad, even if she plays hard to get in Kensington. If she's kind to you in Newtown — Newtown, you know? — then she's interested in you. And if she spurns you in Kensington, that's all right. She wants you to get to know something about her."

"But I'm getting so little writing done," Felix pressed.

"I've told you before, it's not the quantity that counts. It's the genuine inspiration of what you do, coming out of a knowledge of life. That's all that matters."

A girl named Daphne, who had been at The Home, worked near the timber yard and took to dropping by for a chat with Felix. A friend of hers worked at The Home so she sometimes had an item of gossip to impart. It was she who brought the news that Edwin was ill, seriously enough to have been moved from The Home to hospital. Felix got Dad to take him to visit his friend a day or two later. Edwin was scarcely recognizable, unbespectacled, prostrate, and unable to utter more than a breathless word or two. It was the malady that commanded his attention, swelling his abdomen and making him moan and ceaselessly writhe in his bed.

A few days later Felix found himself at one of the de Waal's parties. It was the first in the small house they had moved to — before that they had lived in hotel rooms and a succession of flats — almost a year before, since when Felix had scarcely seen them, understanding that Mr de Waal had been working at an unusual pitch that required him to go into a sort of retreat. Some remnant of quietness still seemed to hang on him during the party, but it did not amount to a dampening of his vivacity nor make him, for Felix, anything less than the vibrant center of things.

"Old Johan is settling down and turning bourgeois these days," Felix was shocked to hear another guest remark to him. "Giving house-warming parties! He's chaining up the demon I used to know, trying to be safe and ordinary now that he's getting a reputation as a respectable author."

The speaker was drunk and Felix put his words down to envy, mischief and blindness. All the same he answered him: "Well, I don't know what he used to be like but I've never come across anyone more alive and free than he is."

"Ag, come off it — you don't really mean that?" the other said with a heavy wink.

"Of course, I do." Felix was indignant. He was about to go on to assert, "A genius knows better than anyone else how to run his life," but held his tongue rather than provoke more sozzled sarcasm, and the exchange ended with a cynical shrug from the man.

A heavy storm took place during the evening, and afterwards when some of the guests were preparing to leave, they found that their cars were bogged down in mud in the yard and along the unpaved street of the new suburb. Some cars pulled away, but there were several, including the one Felix was in, which no amount of engine-racing or pushing could dislodge. Mr de Waal appeared, having changed into khaki shorts for muddy work, and by the light of headlamps through which still streaked a few flecks of rain, set about digging one of the cars free. But although it was strenuous, his effort was in vain, and the guests trooped back inside to resume their seats and eventually try to sleep.

It was known that Mr de Waal had to be at his job in town next morning, yet he and his wife remained in the front room with their guests and tried to rest by bedding down on a table which offered the only sufficient space. Felix saw this as a remarkable courtesy, which some of the other guests, still tipsy and high spirited, seemed not to appreciate, as they went on wisecracking and laughing deep into the night. Mr de Waal meanwhile registered the agonies of fractured sleep with spasmodic and violent jerks and twists on the table, while Felix watched with something like an empathetic agony.

Quiet came at last, and the host was still sound asleep when daylight showed that the ground had dried sufficiently for the gritty-eyed guests to drive away.

On the Monday morning following the Friday of the party, Felix and Dad were eating breakfast and listening to the broadcast news before going to work. Toward the end of the bulletin came the words, "The death has occurred unexpectedly of the well-known South African author, Johan de Waal . . ."

Felix stiffened and took in the remaining words that pressed the message into reality, before he dropped his fork and started wailing: "We killed him . . .Oh, my God! we bloody-well killed him . . ." The news was not new to Dad and Moh. Mrs de Waal had telephoned the previous day to say that her husband had collapsed and died late on Saturday afternoon. They had not known how to break the news to Felix, had meant to prepare him for it.

"I want to go and see her," Felix demanded. So it was arranged that, though incapable of work, he would come to the office and Dad would drive him out to Mrs de Waal in the afternoon.

At mid-morning Daphne appeared. Her message was, "Edwin died on Saturday."

The cemetery was too new to be softened by trees. Stretching to the foot of a low bald ridge, it lay open to the sky. The ridge drew the horizon suffocatingly close and emptied the view of everything but raw veld. It was a place without answers or mysteries, with nothing but bare dumb earth, ready to swallow everything human. No wonder the speeches of tribute to Edwin, one each from a member of committee and an inmate, sounded of nothing but futility. And no wonder none of the many articulate people at Mr de Waal's graveside cared to speak a word of praise in that place.

Standing at the second of the afternoon's two burials, Felix dully noticed Dad's head, unaccustomedly bared for the Gentile rituals, and remembered his fear of sunstroke. He moved a step or two to where he could, with a raised hand, cast a shadow to shield the vulnerable scalp. But for himself he could think of nothing that was left now to temper the blatant emptiness of the sky, the flat banality of the earth.

Moving away from the funeral scene through the following days and weeks, he could not shed that impression. Flat banality seemed to infect the earth since Mr de Waal no longer existed on it. There was the terrible sadness of wasted hope in Edwin's death, and bewilderment and spite in the coincidence of the two deaths — one so close to the self his body made him, the other to the self he aspired to be — but it was Mr de Waal's death that deprived him of his point of reference and cancelled the colour of the world and the possibility of meaning.

He could not write. Not only was his validating reader gone, but so was any reason for writing. But after some months a kind of restoration was started, through the richness of the memory itself. A journal commissioned his recollections of the dead author and he was able to write that article. He became a fascinated audience for reminiscences of anyone he met who had known Johan de Waal; piecemeal memories revealed a history fully as extraordinary as Mr de Waal's personality. There were several unexpectedly sombre strokes in the picture: originality pitched to the point of mental illness, intensity carrying over into criminal violence, and the exacted price of such eruptions. But if Felix discovered these with a feeling of disturbance, he absorbed that feeling into the amazement with which he contemplated the whole brilliant and increasingly mysterious legend of the man.

It was Dad who one day filled in a passage that for a while prevented Felix from holding the image together. "Do you know what I heard about your Mr de Waal from someone in town today? During the war he wrote a letter to a newspaper saying nine million Jewish refugees from Poland wanted to come into this country and they should be allowed in. But he wrote it to make trouble. It wasn't true, he knew there never were so many Jews in Poland. Anyway, his letter caused an outcry, and afterwards the government passed a bill to stop most refugees from coming here."

"Who told you that?"

"A Mr Kaplan, a journalist."

Kaplan was one of the people Felix had met who had known Mr de Waal. The round-about thinking and grandiose scale of that mischief seemed to bear a recognisable stamp.

"Ah, it's bad!" Dad said. "If I knew he did a thing like this I would have had nothing to do with him."

The gentle words — gentle, Felix knew, for his own sake — had the force of a curse on behalf of their injured race. But it was not only that that disconcerted him, nor even the cruel group-selfishness that Mr de Waal was accused of serving with his wit and mordant insight: he could somehow leave the horror of this to his father and others. What confused him more was that Mr de Waal had put his hand to a political machination at all. This was a contradiction that touched something deeper than his morals, which were already complicated beyond the range of judgement. It touched his imaginativeness, his insistence on an individual reality. It robbed his character of some of the unique originality which was its essence, and for the moment left Felix feeling bereaved of Mr de Waal for the second time.

He went to his room and sat a long time at his desk, staring numbly at the broken encyclopedia that stood dominant there because of Edwin and Mr de Waal who had never known each other — he could not remember whether Edwin had been present at the "poyetry" lesson. As for himself, the double or triple knowledge of death that had come through them to him left him feeling that he was irremediably alone and as incapable of using anything he had been taught as if he knew nothing and there was nothing to be known.

"I know nothing . . . I know nothing . . . I know nothing . . ." he muttered, over and over again, until the compulsion of his eyes on the spines of the jumbled volumes affected his tongue, and he began to intone, "L to LOR, SHU to SUB, HAR to HUR, HUS to ITA . . ."

The Moment

Felix was twenty-seven, and nothing had happened
yet. Ten years before he had imagined he could
stop waiting, and had asked Marjory Cane, who was
fifteen, as one would ask for the loan of a cup of
sugar, to lie with him. Adolescents ask questions
of and receive answers from each other by their
lips and finger tips. He had taken none of this
instruction and his naked words were ruder than
any touch. Her repulse left him with too much
shame and fear to feel the thwarting of his desire.

It was the first of many fiascos. Each of these
eruptions threw a crust of shame over his desires.
Later these had settled down into the strata of his
feelings, eventually to compound a suspicion that
the woman's love which alone would let him begin
to be himself would never come to him, that sex,
after all was fiction, a hoax — the suspicion, even,
that he himself did not exist. These doubts and
the tension of his unrequited hunger were growing to a point of unbearable obsession.

In the fifth year after he had abandoned university in mid-course he decided to return and take

his degree. The university setting — with so many lovely bodies in the still-fresh bloom of their responsiveness to each other — brought his frustration to an edge. Each brightly sensuous day that passed seemed overlaid on a flatter and emptier darkness. He was twenty-seven and nothing had happened to him. If another year passed in this way, he felt, he would slide into some kind of madness or even die.

He knew Evelyn Heiner slightly from a series of cultural meetings he and Becky had been attending the year before. She was dumpy, wore her hair in an Eton crop and had not attracted him. Now, after having worked for some years, she had become a student — like him, older than most of the others. During his canteen hours he often found himself in her vicinity because they had a number of friends in common. She was a comfortable person, banteringly voluble, sometimes even uproariously funny.

He was surprised when, with the year well advanced, she sought him out alone one day and asked if she might visit him at home to get his help with one of her assignments. The visit turned out to be brief — a friend with a car brought her and picked her up — and its given reason proved to be a pretext. They spent a few minutes discussing the topic of her essay, and then she produced a piece of verse in which she declared her love for him.

Whatever her offer might mean, the moment dizzied him because it promised a possible end to the waiting that was so exhausting him, and he responded immediately by begging for the permanent rescue: "Will you marry me?"

The request froze her with embarrassment, almost produced one more fiasco. But she had years and ease behind her and laughter to mask the situation. She said, "That's a bit sudden. Let's not talk about marriage. Yet, anyway . . ." She reddened and her voice went low as she spoke the incredible words, "I want us to make love . . ."

There was time for an exchange of urgent kisses to seal a promise, then she left him gyrating in a new universe.

The examination season had begun and they were chained to their books, so in the following weeks she managed only one more brief visit. At first his anticipation filled him with a pleasant tingling relish. It both excited and relaxed him. But as days and weeks mounted, so did his tension. He was increasingly distracted by the reaction of his body, hot and swollen with appetite, and by the knowledge that his lust did not lock him into loneliness and shame, but was to be shared. Yet his desire was not steady and simple. At different times when he looked at Evelyn, the woman promised to him, his desires flared or wavered. One rain-threatened day she appeared at university enveloped in a rumpled dun raincoat and in a raucous mood: she laughed loudly and danced about clumsily on a walk with some friends. He watched her: his girl, bound to him by a poem, a promise and his own desperation. He could feel nothing but reluctance and dismay.

But the desperation was there — reasserting and sharpening itself in this suspended time. He found himself demanding of her on the telephone, "When?" — and the day was fixed for the event she wanted but seemed to have grown to fear.

It was the morning of the last day of November. Behind the closed door of his bedroom, where, he could assure Evelyn, his mother (whatever she might be thinking about the nature of the visit) would not interrupt them, the thing, the thing itself, the actual ultimate event, unromantically but incredibly, even gloriously, took place. While they stripped, before she had removed her dress, she crouched down to the floor and asked him in embarrassment not to watch as she made some necessary intimate preparation. But then she was naked to him. The sight and touchability of her naked body, drugged him. Half outside of his own believable reality he exchanged voracious kisses and caresses with her. His urgency seemed partly to amuse her. Other details also contrived against romance in the final conjunction. He should lie flat, she decided, and she would mount him, to make things easier for him. And during the entry she gasped and moaned with pain, blaming a long spell of celibacy for the inelastic, shrunken condition of her flesh.

But as she came over him and he felt his deepening containment in her body, waves of feeling flushed from his centre to the extremities of his limbs, the top of his head. It was a feeling that was the palpable meaning of romance. The scent of roses, the pleasure he took in the keenest lyrical poetry, came to his mind. He laughed, his whole body, mirthlessly but joyfully, uncontrollably, laughed when his orgasm came. He tried to suppress the convulsions, the silly giggling, snorting, hooting that came from the nets and knots of his nerves and not from his will. But his embarrassment was small against the knowledge that he was saved. Evelyn Heiner had saved him.

During the remaining days of the university term, and through the vacation, she came to give herself to him once or twice a week. Watching her leave him after they had made love, as she crossed to the tram stop, he marvelled that within so short a time after being with him in nakedness and passion she would be sitting indistinguishable among other passengers in the commonplaceness of a tram.

For a long time he remained drunk as much on the thought of at last being a lover as on the passional release. To his parents so much of what he felt and did went untold, but he did let them know — sure they would be happy with him — what Evelyn was to him. The first evening that she stayed for dinner was a Saturday when they, by custom, went to the local cinema. They asked Evelyn and Felix to come as well, but the invitation was awkwardly refused, and the house was left to them. They were quite alone in it for the first time, and were for the first time making total love at night (as distinguished from the feverish exchanges of hampered caresses in dim corners at parties or in motor cars). There was a good freshness, a near beauty, to the full nakedness of her body as she moved through lit and darkened rooms using the freedom of the house to accommodate their love-making.

He was to be again with her by night several times, and for whole nights, moreover. But the snatched two hours of that Saturday evening, at the end of which his father drove her to her boarding house, had an irrecoverable quality of sensual sweetness.

It was her dissatisfaction with her boarding house that led to the beginning of a strain. They had been together several times at an old house in Hillbrow where a friend of his was living in rented rooms. This friend, Joel, had made it clear to Felix that he found Evelyn uncongenial. So when she asked him to recruit Joel's help in getting her a room in the same house, he could not hide his reluctance, and her good nature seemed to evaporate as she sourly reproached, lashed and pressed him. He ended up unhappily yielding a promise to try.

Despite Joel's feelings he complied with the request, and recommended Evelyn to the landlady as one more lodger, and shortly afterwards she did move into the house. It was in that bohemian setting that she became accessible to Felix for night-long visits.

But it was after the first of these visits that Felix was shaken by a surprise flank attack in his emotions. He could not see where to lay the blame: on the fact that now the last detail in the form of romantic possession had been complied with (he had shared the night with his love, had slept with her); or on the possibility that Evelyn had display-ed some reserve in her responsiveness, some new lack of passion in the new situation (she had slept in a long flannel night-dress; had been reluctant to renew lovemaking when they awoke in the morning). But the cause hardly seemed to matter in the face of the feeling itself. The shock was that he was capable of such an emotion. Capable? Incapable was a more appropriate word, for the emotion was emotionlessness. A pervasive feeling of flatness, as though all the solidity, the colour, the juice, had been sucked out of the world. Now that, at last, he had had the whole of his desire, now that fulfilment was at his call, desire had snuffed itself out in him.

Why had no one told him of this possibility? Why had he never read about this experience? It must be because this numbness was some sickness of his own. Everything at last being granted, he, like a spoiled, bored baby, no longer wanted it. But this was no toy. This was sex, love, fruition of his manhood. This cold repulsive ash was life. He had expected that the experience of intercourse would transform him by freeing him from the rigidities of his stale virgin state and from the obsessiveness of his desire: the locks would fall off his manhood and he would become easy and winning with women, and patience would let his energies and imagination out of the strict channel of sexual straining to flow over and open the ne-glected fields of his creativeness. But his knowl-edge of the long-guarded core secret had fed him into a sick slackness and unsluiced his imagina-

tion into sand. After all, after all, for him at least —
being perhaps in his secret heart afraid of what
he had always thought he longed for — there
was nothing to want, and nothing to say.

Inhabiting some other world, Joel had blazoned
among the grafitti on the walls of the kitchen in
that house: "Cunt is king!" To Felix through all
the years it had been the kingdom of heaven, but
now that he was admitted he found a desert of
new shame — he was a hypocrite, a hollow dream-
er, some curious kind of coward — and all-em-
bracing dismay. He stood in a Hillbrow street in
the morning sunlight waiting for a bus to take
him to town on the first stage home. It had not
really been very long since bus riding and access
to the city had been beyond his independent
power. He could remember being unable to walk
. . . All these things had been reached by him, their
mysteries opened to him. Now, staring at the
peopled street, he almost resented whatever had
been granted to him, whatever he knew: the con-
clusion they forced on him was, "So, this is all!"

This new sense of himself persisted, but its
strength was intermittent. It was not strong enough
to immunise him against a jolt of jealousy when
he accidentally learned that on a camping jaunt
with other students, Evelyn had been escorted by
an older man, not a student.

"Evelyn and Samuel Merkle!" he involuntarily
interrupted the girl who was describing the ex-
pedition. "But Evelyn's supposed to be *my* girl . . ."
The three friends present seemed embarrassed —
and he was too, immediately — at this indiscreeet

protest. But he had reacted with a pang, without control.

All the same, when Evelyn confirmed to him that she had become deeply involved with Samuel Merkle, that she was lost to Felix in circumstance as well as in the inadmissible cabinet of his own feelings, the bruise to his pride was salved by his relief at the ending of their affair.

Still, this was too dull and petty a freedom to be relished, and he felt some self-reproach at even thinking of it as a freedom. In any case, the overwhelming upshot of all that had happened was his flat lack of desire. Even the knowledge that it was the turning-off of Evelyn's passion that had desiccated their love-making did not free him from the feeling that the great bluff of his ordinary male aliveness had been called. As the knowing bluffer he might have been cleansed and increased by this hard thrust into truthfulness. But he was the one who had been bluffed — into believing that in himself and in the world he was planted in, there was so much, potential, substantial and sweet, whereas what was there in reality was as tasteless and thin as paper—and he could acknowledge only impoverishment.

And so, on a day not long after the new university year had begun, Felix came to the strangest of moments. A girl walked past him, her lithe legs cupped by the inverted spreading corolla of her skirt. When she had gone, he found his breathing perturbed. A hopeless pang told him that he was re-entering desire, the prison in which he had lain, and certainly would again, an incorri-

gible fool af a detainee, at the mercy of unreach-
able girl after girl. The knowledge was painful, but
he could only welcome it with joy.

Fruits of the Earth

Felix's first, short-lived affair had happened when he was twenty-seven and at a breaking-point, and now there had been six more years without a woman. What counted even more than his physical impediments was a personal deficiency: he froze or frightened the women he loved — or merely wanted — at just the moment when he was attempting persuasion, because he lacked the male knack of acting calmly while impassioned. As for purchasable women, Johannesburg was gruffly secretive about its accommodations (yet, since this was home, could it ever be secretive enough?) and between his timidity and ignorance he had never found his way to them. Six years had brought him again to a point where the needs of his flesh were terrorizing his thoughts.

All at once the European trip was upon him. Gordon and Katherine Slessor were emigrating and they invited him to accompany them on their preliminary tour. It was the time of the Emergency. They'd had to make their decisions suddenly and his notice was brief, but an unusually profitable business deal by Dad just then made it possible for him to go. This was the sort of miraculous opportunity it would be stupid to turn down. Gordon and Katherine could not be bettered as travel-companions and guides. Besides, there was the hint, in some of the names in their itinerary, that this jaunt could becone relevant to his personal emergency. He made the secret acknowledgement that that, in the end, was what he was going for.

They went by sea. The evening before they docked for their half day at Las Palmas, Felix stood with Gordon at the deck-rail listening to his friend's satirical description of what would happen in port: scores of the proper young fellows aboard would stream ashore for their first bit of freedom, and queue up to take their turns with the town's few over-worked tarts. Felix grinned and grimaced at this picture, hiding his dismay.

Next day with Katherine they did the taxi tour of the island and afterwards found they had an hour they could spend in the town. Gordon asked, "What else shall we go and see? The market? Or the cathedral?" He turned to Felix: "Should I get the driver to take you to a brothel?"

Felix avoided looking at Katherine as he stiffly replied, "Not after what you were telling me last night." He knew an aftermath of faint regret over this rejection of his first opportunity, but that evening in conversation Katherine opened to him a set of ideas which filled his thoughts and coloured his feelings during the last days of the voyage. There was for some people, she said, the privilege of a conscious confrontation with suffering, a high, hard fate to embrace if they dared: it was the way, for them, to an extraordinary fulfilment. It could be that for him, she was implying. She was offering him a strange mixture of consolation and cruel challenge. He was moved, inspired almost. By the means she had revealed, he could — and would, he fancied, after all — rise above the riot of himself and refuse the easy compromise solutions.

On the train from Southampton they bought sandwiches and London newspapers and watched through the windows the unfolding of the modest, humane landscape. Katherine and Gordon were palpably filled with satisfaction, with relief almost. Felix could not resist teasing them by pretending that he saw, scrawled on walls in villages, typically South African signs and slogans: "Police State". . . "Let the people vote". . ."Slegs blankes". . ."Gents — Here".

From Waterloo station the taxi route to their hotel took in embankments, bridges, palaces and parks, all bland with the sunshine and greenery of a fine summer noon. Where, Felix wondered, was the great black pit of the London the novelists described? But it was not long before something of that other, darker London of his initial secret anticipation, came mockingly over the scene for him. The Slessors, whose last visit there had been under the shadow of post-war austerity, had a hundred things to remark on, but what fixed his attention in the passing days was their amusement at the prevalence and cunning of prostitutes' advertisements now that street soliciting was suppressed.

He began making explorations on his own, his attention divided between the fable manifest of the city's life and monuments, and the suggestive bits of pasteboard or paper that were supposed to be pinned to doorposts and noiceboards. Somehow — had he missed the favoured area? — the invitations he was looking for eluded him. Or he saw things that were too ambiguous to trust. He pored over screen after screen of blatant photographs outside strip clubs, and one day entered one and sat, with a silent audience in a dark shoebox of a place, through a score of would-be febrile turns, with a hot sense of being near his goal and yet cheated and befouled.

At last he found the formula he expected and made his way up three flights of battered stairs, only to be turned away by a suspicious old hanger-on who insisted that "Madam does not work to-day."

Paris would, must, be different. It was. The Slessors seemed to find its beauty richer and more moving. After their first supper in their hotel on the Ile de la Cité, the pair of them took a long walk to revisit some specially remembered scenes, leaving Felix to settle in his room and explore the immediate vicinity. When they returned Katherine went to bed, but Gordon offered to go out again and show Felix a little of what there was to be enjoyed.

They drank coffee at a sidewalk table in the Place St Michel where they could see the fountain and glimpse, above the roofs, the top of Notre Dame itself. But the setting and the cosmopolitan throng taking the balmy air amid the lights were to Felix a mere papery phantasmagoria obscuring the single elusive reality. As they started back toward the hotel, he said to Gordon, "Please tell me, where are the red lights?"

Gordon looked faintly affronted and embarrassed. "There aren't actually red lights . . ." he said, and a silence fell between them.

The museums and restaurants, the marvels and monuments and shrines he visited during the next few days left Felix chilled, unbelieving, finally hysterical. The more he saw the more he felt the unreality of things and of himself. He moved for hours among silent Rembrandts and Chardins in the Louvre, oppressed by the dull suspicion of some terrific deception somewhere — perhaps in himself, perhaps in the long-awaited masters. But it was the Seine, endlessly varying the reflections of chestnut avenues, palaces, moulded balustrades and bridges, that, because it had the elements of what should be an ultimate loveliness, was the worst, the most desolating of all.

On the fifth evening he took a long ramble with Gordon and Katherine on the Right Bank. Somewhere beyond Les Halles among crooked narrow streets, they saw a woman standing at the kerb, exposed like a statue, her arms folded, a bag dangling from one wrist, her foot beating placid time to the tune she absently hummed. "There's a tart," Gordon remarked. They turned the corner she was standing at, and the next street was revealed as a marketplace of waiting women and hovering circumspect men.

The scene realised an ancient fantasy of Felix's, long since abandoned as improbable. And yet he walked through the place with a strained aloofness, feeling, despite his friends' amusement at the various miniature comedies of strutting and ogling, banter and haggling, a certain shame before them. After a while his awkwardness seemed to be communicated to them and they grew quieter. He wondered uneasily whether Gordon had told Katherine about his mistimed request of the first evening. If so, she would be aware of his hidden excitement over the commerce they were witnessing and of the defection — possibly it was also a kind of betrayal— that it implied. It humiliated him to be exposed — and equally, to have failed.

Nevertheless, two evenings later (it was his earliest opportunity) he set out alone to find that street again. Vague about how they had arrived there, he wandered for nearly an hour without finding the place. He was beginning to feel exasperated when he came not to that street but another, wider, brighter, with hotels sporting illuminated signs, cafés from which music came, and gayer men and prettier, more flamboyant women parading what was less ambiguously a place of pleasure. One girl of a surprisingly proud, fastidious style of good looks — dark and petite and dressed in crisp yellow with a spread skirt that swayed like a bending flower about her slender legs as she paced — drew him. He went happily toward her.

"S'il vous plaît . . ." he said, but she passed him without acknowledgement. Either she had not heard him or he had, after all, mistaken her. In fact she was too good in the part to be true. But then he saw her speak to a man and go with him into an hotel. In barely fifteen minutes she was back outside, and almost immediately, before Felix could go up to her, another man approached and she went inside with him.

Felix waited at the hotel door and stepped in her path as she emerged. "Bon soir, Mademoiselle," he said, and she met him with an immobile look. "Je voudrais . . ." he pointed at her, at himself, and turned his lips into a smile. But she shook her head and began to walk away. "Pourquoi?" he called. "Qu'est-ce que? Combien? Oh, God, I've got enough money . . ."

But she was away, oblivious, the poppy of her skirt swinging with her freedom to take and refuse as she pleased, round a corner out of his view. A minute later he was still dazedly staring after her, anxious to press his right, to argue it out, when she reappeared at the corner. She halted there when she saw him and gave one more faint shake of her head. Then she crossed the road to where there was a knot of other women. They stared at him and talked among themselves. Then one of them, a tall black woman, came over to him. Close before him she stopped and looking in his face nodded gravely like a child.

He felt very weary and remained silent for several seconds, staring bitterly at the girl in yellow. Then half fiercely and half mechanically he said,

"Combien?"

Quaintly the woman leaned forward and whispered, "Quatre mille." Her price was her secret and their intimacy had begun. Beginning to see her voluptuousness, the piquant ironies of her offer, he nodded and followed where she led. Through a doorway they came to a thickly carpeted staircase with a polished banister. But it was narrow and steep, and halfway up the first flight there was a sharp turn and a tread which afforded only a toehold. He needed a little help and put his hand out toward the woman. "S'il vous plaît . . . Votre main."

She stopped and looked back at him. He stretched toward her the hand he wanted her to seize, but she made no move.

"Le main," he said. Was that the right word? "Votre main, si'l vous plaît. Assistez moi . . ."

A small sound came from her as she stared at him, but she remained unmoving.

"Votre main," he groaned, scraping the air with his own hand, and she gave a sort of giggle and muttered, "J'ai peur," the meaning of which he did not remember.

"Just give me your hand," he begged. "Si'l vous plaît, votre main . . ." And then he understood what it was that she was saying, in a squeaky whisper like an incipient scream, over and over again, "J'ai peur . . . Ooh, j'ai peur . . ." Frightened. She was afraid of him.

His air was wild when he got back downstairs to the street, and three women in succession simply turned away as he approached them. After the third bid he walked desperately away from that street.

In a place that was empty of people he stopped, his face pressed against a darkened shop window, and stood motiveless for a long time. At last the thought came of returning to the hotel on the Ile and going to sleep. But the thought of that sleep made him more frightened than the woman paralysed on the staircase. If this was how he had to return and go to sleep, with the world all ice and stone and a joke, he would never feel real again. Yet he had done the thing, made the demand, gone all his share of the way, already. What was there left for him to do?

Still, when he at last began again to walk, it was northwards, away from the river. After some blocks he came to another of the prostitutes' beats. It was an ill-lit street with dingy buildings, and the women too seemed shadowy and dingy. Intimidated and drained of lust, he walked slowly along, incapable of action or decision.

None of the figures he saw stirred his desire. Here and there his eye recognised a symbol of enticement — a swing of hair or skirt, a half-bare breast — but it sent through him only a tremor of hopelessness.

Two blocks down, the street was nearly deserted, but he walked idly on toward the next corner. Rounding it he saw what seemed one last, remote patch of activity. A few girls loitered near a couple of opaque doorways, their flesh and the shadows different shades of grey. Over the road several more sat at tables outside a small drab café.

Felix stopped and leaned against a wall, watching passively. It was late and growing cold.

At first it seemed that a strange stillness lay upon the street, as though the women and the three or four ruminating men had strayed here by mistake and were suspended like him in indifference. One man hung quite immobile save for a hand and a cigarette. Two others exchanged muttered remarks. One walked with surreptitious slowness past several of the women and when he paused by one it seemed that a single subdued gurgle of laughter was all that heralded his disappearance with her into the maw of a building.

There was a flicker of movement when one woman ran across the road to the café and spoke to those who were sitting there. They responded with some argument and laughter and after a minute or two she re-crossed and went to stand with a tall, copper-haired girl to whom she made some animated comments. Felix began to focus his attention on the full-fleshed looks of the redhead. She gestured at her high-heeled shoes and said something briskly, and the other, with a grin, ran back to the café.

The redhead gave Felix a passing glance, and he prepared to approach her, but at his decision his breath began to race as though he had exerted himself. While he waited for it to quieten, the messenger returned from the café. She must be some servant or exploiter of the other women, he supposed; she was dressed differently, in denim jeans and a colourless jersey, and since her hair was shingled she seemed to have put aside her woman's guise. He came nearer to the pair, hoping to catch the redhead's eye again.

But his guess was wrong. A man—a middle-aged Oriental in a sports jacket and an open khaki shirt, carrying a sandwich-tin—walked without loitering straight up to the girl in jeans, and seemingly without a word between them, she led him through a nearby doorway.

Felix waited a few minutes before gathering himself to move toward the redhead and speak. But abruptly he became aware that someone else was within a yard or two of him and coming nearer. It was the silent smoking man, a big dark-haired young fellow whose blue suit pulled across the muscles of his arms and legs. He seemed to be staring closely at Felix from behind his dark glasses. Felix waited for him to go away. But the man stayed, a small muscle working in one of his sallow-skinned cheeks, his fingers trembling as they carried his cigarette from his small bluish mouth. At last he spoke.

"Je ne parle pas francais," Felix answered.

The man repeated his first remark, then made another.

Felix explained again that he did not understand, but the man remained there speaking insistently to him. He did not seem drunk.

A minute later the girl in jeans emerged from the doorway and the Chinese walked away as silently as he had come. For a few moments she watched the young man speaking to Felix, then she spoke sharply to the young man. He glared at her, shrugged and walked away.

"Are you English?" she asked Felix.

"Yes."

"Tourist?"

He nodded.

"Where is your hotel?"

"Ile de la Cité."

"So far! This is the quartier Algérien. It is dangerous for you. That man wanted to make trouble." Felix saw that she was not at all masculine.

He said, "Thank you."

She nodded, then, "What do you want here?" she asked.

"You," Felix said.

She looked at him for a moment in silence, as though not immediately understanding, then solemnly nodded again, and taking his arm led him inside, up a naked old stairway—and into a cell of a room where there was a bed starkly covered with a plastic sheet, a hand-wash basin, and a bidet.

"Please," she said when they arrived, "Five new francs for the room. And twenty francs for me." The price was humble, and the blank way she named it was even more so. It made him momentarily recall the solemn-faced Chinese who had silently come to her and gone again, with the sad quiet sureness of routine. Felix paid her and they undressed only sufficiently and with no kiss or caress came together. It was abrupt and mechanical, yet urgent and reverberating. She let him lie a full minute when the release had come, breathing in grateful stillness. The ablutions afterwards celebrated rather than brought about his cleansing. As they dressed they talked a little, asking for each other's names and origins. When they were ready he thanked her fervently. She, with an unexpected matching fervour, kissed him on the cheek.

Down in the street she urged him to take a taxi for his safety's sake, and he half promised that he would if he should see one. But the midnight streets were empty until he neared Les Halles. There he saw no taxis, but a tide of other life. The area was bustling with the preparations for the morning's trade. Everywhere there were marketeers arguing and hallooing and chalking out the positions of their stalls, like claims on a diamond diggings. Restaurants were open and busy. He entered one where some market women were gossiping at the counter over little glasses of black steaming liquor. He took an onion soup. This, of course, as the Slessors had reminded him, was the famous time and place for it. It was good. While he ate he watched the lively old women at the counter. They were joined by some newcomers whose orders told him that the black drink was mere "café", made festive by the glasses.

When he had finished the vast scalding bowl of soup and left the restaurant, the activity outside was at a pitch, the streets almost blocked by people, barrows, handcarts, piles of gaping crates spilling reds and greens and whites and yellow and purple, and shunting lorries with new freights of dusty dry stuff and juicy perishable produce turning the city's night into the whole cycle of seasons for the burgeoning and reaping of a brief prodigious harvest. Through the maze of it all Felix's path was difficult and even dangerous. But he picked his way, beyond all fear, exulting amid many-scented pyramids of the fruits of the earth.

Are You Sick?

Felix thought he glimpsed the girl again (he had forgotten her name!) one afternoon when he was waiting for someone at the entrance to African Arts House. This southern end of town was predominantly black, and watching the crowds of pedestrians that streamed along the pavements, as factories, offices and shops closed, he had a sudden inkling of the black man's Johannesburg: it was larger, fuller, more multi-layered than the white city, and, yes, more open in its possibilities, like London or Paris.

But the girl's momentary appearance, if it was she, contained a denial of possibilities. Dozens of people passed him, entering or leaving the building. This one, a shortish shapely figure dressed in white with a smart beret, having come from behind him down the stairs, swung onto the pavement and sheered away keeping her face averted. Usually people paused as they emerged from the building, at least glanced to his side. He had thought he might cross her path there one day and had wondered, a little apprehensively, what would happen. Slipping past him like that, she let

207

him off easily, in a sense. But he did feel disturbed. He hadn't thought before of her as needing to avoid the sight of him, being hurt herself . . .

The thing had begun at one of Robin Henderson's notorious parties two years before. Moh and Dad were abroad at the time visiting Becky, who had married and emigrated. Felix had the house to himself. More important, this meant he was on his own, unattached, unwatched and utterly free, as he had been only once before in his life, in Europe. This was the first time he was nakedly face to face with Johannesburg, with himself at home. The sense of his liberty, to explore neglected possibilities, to indulge whims usually checked, went to his head.

The mood at the party suited his. The detention-without-trial law had just been promulgated, and some of the guests were politicals who felt themselves about to be destroyed. If they set the tone of a final carefree night, it was caught up and amplified through all the crowded rooms of the house. At least half the guests were blacks — journalists, actors and musicians from African Arts House with their friends, including, as Dan later told Felix, not a few prostitutes — and everyone seemed to be drinking, dancing and bellowing under the bellowing music with a sort of angry energy of abandon.

Felix had on three evenings in the previous fortnight made his way by bus to a fringe of town that was desolate after nightfall, and walked eight blocks to a building in Jeppe Street which someone long before had pointed out to him, in amusement, as a brothel. The women who clustered around the doorway seemed, like fishmoths, products and prisoners of what they inhabited. No more than the mean spec-built block were they there in a spirit of fun, glamour or tradition, but purely for commerce. Still, the girl who took him up to her room was patient and wore perfume, so he filled himself with waves of tenderness for her and fancied that if he'd had an unlimited supply of money he would have gone to her every day. In fact, in terms of what he had, the amounts he had to pay her were extravagant enough to give his indulgence a twist of perversity. He felt freed and also imprisoned by that ugly, grimy building.

What the party seemed to be promising him was both a contrast and a complement to the brothel. Because he could not dance and was therefore an observer, he could preserve no detachment but yielded himself to the heady licentiousness of the atmosphere. For hours, however, he was uncomfortable — tantalized by his feeling of readiness. He drifted from room to room, catching glimpses of his particular friends, Gloria, Dan, Norma, all of whom seemed that night involved in more or less painful exchanges, stricken and distracted. Eventually he sat on a sofa beside a girl he knew slightly; she had an inviting body and a free manner. They began speaking, bantering. Then a man came, sat next to her, murmured a few phrases and put his arm around her. After a few seconds their mouths came hungrily together . . .

Then she was there, next to Felix on the other

side. One of the African girls. Not one of the conspicuously febrile ones who wore wigs or satiny headscarves knotted tight and low over the eyebrows, whose tireless vigorous dancing redoubled the stupifying impact of the blast from the music tape speaker, but still, one of the black girls. She had a demure heart-shaped face and wore a hat, like a suburban matron at church. A man had been dancing repeatedly with her earlier on; now he was out of sight, very probably knocked out by liquor.

She was discussing something in vernacular with two other girls standing nearby. As though disentangling herself she turned her face away from them toward Felix, and after a few moments they drifted away.

"How you, honey?" she asked him.

"Fine, thanks . . ."

"Having a good time?"

"Okay and you?"

"I'm having a great time, sweetie . . ." She was pressing herself against him. He put his hand and forearm against her back.

"What's your name?" she asked. He told her and asked for hers.

She pressed closer and whispered, "Do you like me, sweetheart?"

"Yes . . ."

They sat in the semi-dark and fondled each other surreptitiously.

"Can I come and see you?" Again a whisper.

"Yes, yes."

"Do you live alone?"

"Yes, for the time being. My family is away."

"What about the girl?"

"Who? Oh, the servant . . . She finishes in the morning."

"Where do you live?"

He named the suburb, then sat wondering.

"I like you so much, big boy."

"I like you too . . ."

The lights went out for a minute. In the dark they were free. Her caresses were cunning . . . Later she fetched a scrap of paper and wrote his address down.

As soon as he had the house to himself the next Monday, after the housemaid had finished her dusting and laundering, he drew all the curtains. She was to come at three. She was out of a job. He waited on the front verandah so that he could let her in without delay and reduce the chance of her being seen entering the house. One part of his mind disbelieved that she would come, even though she had telephoned him the day before just to exchange loverlike assurances and hints about the pleasures to come.

He was hungry for her, and also needed her because what was promised was a personal exchange and not a cold expensive transaction. And the piquancy that came from his extravagance at the brothel would not be missed; it would be more than replaced by her being black and doubly or trebly forbidden. At the same time he was frightened, skittish as a new burglar, stretched taut with anxiety over the risks he was taking for his family, the house, himself. He could only take them, he thought, because she was taking similar chances to be with him.

There she was, smart in white, with handbag, high heels and a beret, seeming conspicuous because a well-dressed African woman was not a common sight in the white suburban street. And she was smiling at him, carefully but warmly. He managed a stiff momentary smile back. As she reached him he shooed her through the open doorway and slammed the door shut behind them. Inside he took her into his arms immediately, thrust his body against hers and his tongue deep into her mouth, opening his lips to feel the thickness and brownness of hers.

At last she drew her face free. "You in a hurry!" she laughed.

"I can't wait."

"No, but darling, I'm hungry. I want to eat something first."

They went into the kitchen and he found her a meal which she ate at leisure while they chatted with a relaxed flirtatiousness which was strange to him because it was so different from what his imaginings had been during that weekend. Two or three times as she watched him move about the kitchen she exclaimed, to herself, not to him, "Auw, shame!" It was the reflex sympathy of a complete stranger and for a moment made them oddly remote from each other and the state of being lovers. But he let it pass without protest, and the only thing that disrupted the loving mood was his confiding in her, "My God, you know, but I'm frightened."

"Of what?"

"Of getting caught."

It offended her. "Ah, no. Why d'you say that? I can also get caught."

"Yes of course, I know. But . . ."

"No, don't talk like that!"

He was surprised. On this point of their danger especially he had expected complete understanding, but as he tried to explain his fear, it became almost as though he were somehow flaunting his whiteness at her, insulting her colour — at least blaming it for placing him in danger. He let the subject be dismissed for then, but his nervousness was too real and oppressive to stay forgotten or unspoken for long.

When she had eaten her fill they went to his bedroom, dim as a tent because of the drawn curtains, and began to embrace and kiss.

"Do you like me, honey?" she murmured. "Do you love me, really?"

"Yes, yes." he said, nuzzling her. "I want you, my darling, my love. I've been waiting and waiting for you. I want you now . . . Please . . ."

"Let me undress," she said. And then, "You sure the girl won't come in again?"

"Yes, I'm sure. She's finished for the day. And even if she knocks at the door I won't let her in — she'll think I've gone out."

"She hasn't got a key?"

"No."

Later it struck him as a strange thing that the only fear she showed had to do with the servant, the people in the yard. Africans — about whom he was least worried.

She began to strip. Her underclothing was elaborate: stockings, suspender belt, brassiere. He stared thirstily as her naked body emerged, honey-brown, firmly plumped out, with high buttocks, yet petite, making him think of pictures of Bushmen. She giggled. "Am I nice, sweetheart?"

"Yes. God, yes . . ."

"Ooh, you big. So nice and big."

They had plenty of time. Time in which to make love ferociously, wild with their sense of the taboos they were breaking; then time in which to doze, to talk and play, to rest and renew desire and give satisfaction another and another chance. Body to body they grew kindlier, closer as the hours passed, though in their words they remained strangers. Repeatedly they asked for romantic reassurances.

"Say you love me."

"I love you, darling."

"Do you think I'm beautiful?"

"Yes, yes."

She questioned him about himself, sometimes unanswerably. Did he have a girl friend? Why wasn't he married? Why didn't he tell his father to get him a wife?

"Do you read all these books? You must be very clever."

Another time it was a question that surprised him even more.

"Did you ever make love with African girls before?"

In his turn he asked her, "Have you been with other white men?"

"Yes."

"One, or more than one?"

"More than one. Quite a few. Also some boys." These were schoolboys at a boarding school who would come from their dormitory at night to make love with her among the bushes on a nearby koppie. He could imagine how they thought and talked of her in that dormitory. Yet "make love" was the only expression she used. To her, her embraces with those boys were acts of virtue.

"Weren't you frightened?"

"Yes. But they like to make love with me."

But at other moments she seemed naively grasping and scheming. She kept falling into the phrases and attitudes of glossy magazines, and every now and again she made a sudden definite demand.

"Haven't you got a jersey to give me?"

"No, but I'll get you one."

"Will you, sweetheart? A present for me? Thank you, honey."

Then it was, "Can't you find me a job? Oh, I need a job. Please get a job for me."

"Well, I'll watch out. But I don't know anyone who could employ you."

"Hasn't your father got a business? Oh, you must ask him to give me a job ... Will you, please?"

"Well, I'll see ... But ..."

"Gee, if I worked for you, sweetheart, we could make love every day."

He laughed.

"Why do you laugh?"

"Secret love-making every day."

"Yes. Do you like that?"

"It would be too good to be true," he said tipsily, beginning to fondle her. "I would love to have you every day. Wouldn't you get tired of me?"

"Oh never, honey. You so nice. You do it to me so good . . ."

"Not good enough yet," he said. "I still want to try and give you your pleasure. I come too quickly."

"Sweetheart, you my lover, my best lover, so nice." She was answering him, searching caress for caress. His used flesh began to stir again. He mouthed her lips, her ear, her breasts.

"My darling," she whispered, "you must help me to go away from South Africa, to Northern Rhodesia, then you must come there and marry me."

He broke away from her. "You're a funny girl. Is that what you really think of? We don't know each other yet."

She seemed indignant. "Why do you say we don't know each other? We making love, aren't we? Why you say that? I know you. You my lover."

"Yes, of course . . . But that isn't all —"

"Auw! What do you say now? You don't love me."

"But I do, I do. Look at me sweetheart, look at my body. I want you, I need you so much." He pressed close to her again, but she kept her face averted though he murmured coaxingly to her. "Don't you believe me? I find you so lovely, so exciting . . . Oh I want you now, now. See how ready I am . . . I love you, I love you."

He drew her hand onto himself and she let it

stay, then feather-lightly began to fondle him. For minutes at a time they knew nothing but each other's flesh. He felt he was dissolving into her. It was the completest love-making, body to body (but did this qualification mean anything?), that he had ever experienced.

It was drawing toward the time for her to go. The gloom in the room had deepened. He put on a light and dressed while she went to the bathroom to wash.

"Oh, you got lovely soap," she said when she came back half-dressed. "It smells so nice."

"That scented stuff . . . I think there's a new cake somewhere. I'll give it to you."

"Thank you, sweetheart," she said, sitting beside him and caressing his shoulder almost shyly. "You so good to me."

"Well, you're so good to me."

"We good together."

"Yes . . ." he kissed her cheek.

"Can I always come here to make love with you, sweetheart?"

"You're coming on Thursday, for the whole night . . ."

"But I mean always . . ."

"Always, my darling, any time for the next two months. But after that my parents will be coming back . . ."

"I can come with other people. You can say we are your friends . . ."

"No . . . No, it wouldn't work . . ."

"Why?"

"But, my dear, what we're doing is already so

dangerous."

"You frightened?"

"Yes. Yes, of course."

"Why you frightened more than me?" She spoke with suspicion and indignation. Again he felt bewildered: she really seemed not to know his point of view, and he couldn't explain it without seeming to insult her.

"It's dangerous. I want you as long as I can have you even though I'm frightened as it is. But when they come back it will be impossible. Can't you see that? It just is so . . ."

"No," she said. "I can't understand what you saying . . ." And then she was weeping. "I want you for ever, but you don't love me." Her tears continued without words and her looks grew more bitter and disconsolate while he, feeling both trapped and guilty, could not without making himself a liar move to comfort her or answer her accusation.

He stood over her watching her face with incredible tears chasing each other down her cheeks, and pleaded pointlessly, "What's the use of telling you lies? Making you promises I can't keep? Please, tell me what's really the matter. I want you very much, you know how much I enjoy making love with you. You're the best I've ever had. Oh, hell . . ."

During her meal she had first spoken of her need of a job and had added that she was short of money. He had promised to give her some. Now he was thinking about that promise. It looked as if her heartbroken mood was going to persist, as if nothing more could pass between them but their goodbyes and she would go away on this same tide of bitter withdrawal. She must dress and collect her things; they must wind up whatever had to be done. If he was to keep his promise he must do something about it now. But he hesitated to give her the money while she was still weeping, in case she misread him as trying to buy off tears, adding insult to whatever harm he had already done. He watched her put on her stockings and underclothes, her skirt, her blouse, keeping her face averted all the time from his. At last he fetched £2 and pushed it apologetically into her hand. Immediately she stopped weeping. "Oh, thank you, honey." She smiled as though this were all she had been waiting for.

In her new cheerful mood she turned her attention to his tape recorder which had earlier aroused her curiosity. "Ah, honey," she pleaded, "let me sing you a song on your recorder."

He was reluctant to create mementos, but her tears had cowed him, so he gave in as soon as she pouted. Her song was a mawkish love ballad which she crooned, meaning every word, in an American accent. He listened restlessly, feeling unreal, embarrassed, almost impatient for her to go. But he praised her voice and she told him she had sung in African Arts concerts and dreamed of starring in a big show and becoming famous like Miriam Makeba.

When she was dressed they went to the kitchen for some milk and cheese and biscuits. He gave her the tablet of scented soap and a slab of chocolate. At the front door they had a last light kiss.

"Thursday, sweetheart . . ." she said.

"Yes, Thursday. I'll be waiting for you." He meant it.

He ushered her through the door, closed it to a slit and watched her go along his path and fumble at his tricky gate and walk out into the anonymous nightlit street.

Once he was alone his thoughts turned in on him. It was too much of an adventure, too much like a night fantasy, and not even strictly his own. What had happened to his skin and senses became dreamlike, and at the same time the risks he had been asserting moved down from the level of verbal realities to his senses, so that the implications of the past hours blew on him like wind on a naked skin. He grew giddy with danger and unreality. She could be anything — what did he know about her? For all he knew she might be a police trap, or a blackmailer, or a prostitute who meant to milk him of as much as she could. (How he'd played into her hands by declaring his terrors!) At best she was a sloppy nymphomaniac, vulgar and neurotic, an unreal sentimentalist with whom he had nothing in common, whom he could only hurt or be hurt by. He had been reckless, irresponsible, naive. It was suicidal.

Or was she life?

On that chance, once he had emerged from his panic, he held fast to the thought of Thursday, and the other days there would be for two months to come. The morning after her visit he went to town. He cashed a cheque, bought a woman's olive green cardigan and, though he had no need of a haircut, visited a barber's where he had seen the owner sell prophylactics from a cache among the hair oils, razor blades, watch straps and combs.

That evening he saw Dan. As much out of habit as urgency he disburdened himself to him. It was a fearful secret for anyone to be loaded with. Dan was about the last person Felix would want to trouble, but about the only one whom he could tell this thing. "There's so much about it that I want and need," he said, "but I'm scared stiff." He wasn't intentionally asking for advice — rather talking under compulsion, looking for some relief in talk itself.

Dan said, "You must get out of it, end it as soon as you can." Dan was not a simple person; he rarely saw things so simply. But this time what was needed lay beyond complication and question. Felix felt relief in accepting the advice as the only sane course. He would end the relationship with the girl, at the first opportunity, at any cost. Relationship? After all, what he had was only another expensive transaction, deceptively frilled. And a deadly one at that.

He never afterwards questioned the rightness of Dan's advice. Short of being in Felix's experience, no, in his actual physical skin, Dan was right, indubitably right for the sake of safety (not only Felix's own), sanity, everything. But his skin and hers had stroked and warmed each other, been intimately pressed together, sweated and sweetened together, pore against pore and hair into hair, that unhurried loving afternoon.

So, though he hadn't hesitated in assenting to Dan's admonition, he was glad with his skin, so to speak, that there was still to be Thursday, the bounty of hours from evening to dawn (when she would leave by one of the earliest buses so as to be away before the servant was up) to fill with their last love-making — since it would be pointless, cruel perhaps, to dismiss her as she arrived: he had the impression her journey between her home and his was a long one. He still had Thursday in store and was glad he had prepared for it.

But on Wednesday afternoon she telephoned him. "Hello, sweetheart. How's my darling?"

"Look," he said, "it's no good. We can't go on. You mustn't come."

"What? Tomorrow?"

"Not tomorrow. Not any time. We can't carry on."

"Auw! What's the matter? Don't you like me?"

"It's not that. It's just too dangerous."

"Why now? What's the matter?"

"If you don't know, I can't explain. We just must stop. I can't carry on." She was silent and might have been crying. "I'm very sorry," he said.

"What's the matter?" she asked again, with a different sort of curiosity. "Are you sick?"

He did not know just what she meant, yet he might have adopted that explanation. It was a way of blanketing his behaviour, softening the rejection. But he couldn't. "Sick . . . No, I'm not sick. I can't explain. We just can't go on."

"You sick . . ."

"No. Please. It's just finished. I'm sorry."

And that was that. End of story. He told Dan how it had happened and they shared the relief that the chapter was safely closed. He gave the olive green cardigan to the servant. After some weeks he went to Jeppe Street again. The girl he had been having was away that evening. He took one of the others.

Cut Glass

On each of the two days Felix sustained a small cut, the first on his forefinger, the second on his thumb. The last signs of them were healed in a week. Perhaps it was simply adult life — no less than it was child's life — to oscillate across the sharp divide between reality and unreality and receive the occasional injury.

The episodes were minor. They occurred while his parents were abroad, and he, at his choice, was staying alone at home, making, in a sense, his first naked confrontation with the city. Some friends' jocular reference, as they had driven along the easterly stretch of Jeppe Street, had identified a greasy-looking black-and-brick three-storeyed block as a brothel, and Felix had eventually, one evening, essayed the bus journey and the seven-blocks' walk to confront what the place had to offer. He had been lucky at first, for the girl who presented herself in response to his inarticulate signals and took him up to her room was pleasant-natured and patient. In some unvoiced way she accommodated their personalness in the mechanical situation. When he returned — he found himself wishing he could do so daily — he regularly asked for her, and took to bringing her little gifts, to turn what passed between them into something better than a transaction.

He found that business went on at the brothel during the afternoons as well as the evenings, and the daylight jaunt was usually more convenient for him. But one afternoon his regular mate was not to be found, so, with hardly a tic of compunction, he took the service of another girl. She turned out to be stiff and remote, unfriendly in the nervous self-addressed exclamations she gave at his caresses. In future, perhaps, he thought, he would forego the gratification — even after the journey — if the right girl were not there.

The series of his visits was interrupted for a few weeks because of a more fulfilling and intimate adventure. When that was over and he resorted to Jeppe Street again he found that "his" girl no longer took a room there, and the others he spoke to could not tell him where to find her. So he abandoned his resolution, and went with the first girl who made herself available to him. His visits, after that, were irregular, and his rewards uneven. Once he found a thin redhaired girl, apparently new to the building, who clinched her deep admission of him with a vigorous pressure of thighs, belly and loins which he found sharply delicious. Either she was a mistress of technique, or the voluptuary completeness came from the accidental fitting of their bodies. He would have liked her service again, but had not asked for her name. He glimpsed her once more several visits later, but she was sitting on a step, her mouth bleeding, yelling obscenities at someone invisible, apparently drunk.

Usually his encounters amounted to drab, awkward commerce. The place itself yielded nothing to colour or soften it. Some of the rooms were occupied by pensioners and indigent families: often there were children at play about the lobby, passages and staircase, and they seemed simply knowing about the business of the building. He wondered dully about the harm to them that he might be contributing to. But that was momentary. He tried to lace the whole serial of his custom there with a tincture of luridness by the thought of his promiscuousness ranging from woman to woman.

The day he nicked his finger eluded even this colouring. It marked the low point in the series and the beginning of its end (to which he resigned himself a bare month later, after the day he found the place unusually quiet and clean and his way blocked by an elderly woman with a look of authority who met his request for Marion with a contemptuous, threatening, dismissive jerk of her head). That was all there was to it, really. He could not hide from himself the fact that this visit was only squalid. He arrived at the building in a little turmoil of dark feeling, that was really no more than readiness for routine placation, at an earlier hour than ever before — the afternoon was still callow after the lunch break. One woman only lounged in the doorway and he could see no others in the lobby beyond her. She was rather older, grosser, shabbier than most of the girls he usually saw there, and although she immediately assented to his mumbled proposition, she seemed somehow disconcerted, vaguely unready.

He was usually taken to one of the rooms on the first floor, but this time he had to climb higher, and it was on the second staircase that he passed a grimy window with a missing pane. He put his hand where the emptied steel frame offered him a more convenient leverage for his climb than closed window and blank wall, and it was there that a chip of glass, still embedded in the old putty and almost hidden in sooty dust, scratched a shred of skin from his forefinger. Only the dirt made him give the injury a second thought. He'd apply a disinfectant as soon as he got home.

He was always sticky with perspiration in that building after the walk from the bus stop, and on this hot day he was having to climb yet another flight above the second floor. At the top was an open door to the outside. They emerged on the tarmac of the roof area with a block of servants' rooms in the centre. There were several Africans about. One or two of them regarded him and spluttered with giggles of surprise and derision. The prostitute ignored these, exchanged a word with one of the others, produced a key and opened the padlock on the door to one of the rooms.

If this was her home there were signs that a man — her husband? — shared it with her. A jacket of his was draped on a hanger behind the door. Flustered, hot, confused in his feelings about the setting, Felix took what the woman, somehow wearily, gave him of her body. While upon her he noticed a rankness which overwhelmed the smells of the room and of his sweating skin. It was a stink that clung first for hours to his own body, then for weeks in his imagination. This particular conjunction with another person seemed what such an event, he had thought, could never be: less meaningful than masturbation.

He had an invitation to lunch next day with his aunt. Auntie Sarah was the white-haired widow of Dad's brainy brother, Lewis, the daughter of a rabbi and the mother of two serious, brainy, academic children. Her life was replete with calamities, tragedies even, but she mother-of-pearled them with the stoicism of her silence about them, and the sheeny enamel of unflawed respectability in the order of her existence. Respectability had been the essential spirit of her home since his earliest memories of it, when his boisterously intellectual uncle—now sixteen years dead—and earnest cousins had been with her, still admired as scholars and connoiseurs. Respectability was a stuffy, fussy, superficial attribute—but there was something incongruously strong in the way she had sustained it long after exile and death had robbed her of those three who had contributed to its substance. She had been left "comfortably off", and no doubt that had eased her way, but it did not empty the force of what, so unforcedly (with her petite physique and nervous tentative manners) she represented.

His conversations in her house long ago had always been with one of those three members of her family. What passed between Felix and her was not substantial discussion but a tissue draped on polite enquiries about health, schooling, literary activities. It had hardly ever happened that he was her lone guest. But, as always, she had a slender stream of solicitous questions and comments on family and neutral matters.

"How are you managing alone at home? Does your girl cook? You must have proper meals. It's important for your health. Don't you want to take your jacket off? It's a hot day. But at least it's not like the khamseen in Israel. That kind of heat I found unbearable. I could hardly breathe. But if that was the only trouble they had there I would be grateful. Oh, those fedayeen! Shooting at a school on a kibbutz, injuring children. It breaks my heart to think of poor Israel. The trouble never seems to end . . . " (Her surviving son lived there.) They listened to the broadcast news together and she tutted apprehensively or deploringly at the various dangers and wickednesses at large in the world.

He was left to scan Uncle Lewis's knowledgeably chosen objets d'art (this watercolour was a Maris; could that tiny engraving actually be a Rembrandt?), the eclectic bookshelves (Nietzsche, Marx, Freud, Wells, Shakespeare . . .), the showcase with its two never-touched tea sets and its restrained assortment of somehow unaccountable ornaments (china shepherdess, meticulously dressed Geisha doll: could these have been his uncle's choices?); then to sprawl awhile on the anti-maccassared settee over a newspaper — while Aunt Sarah busied herself with her African maid in the faintly gassy kitchen, before serving the meal.

As they ate, her streamlet of talk flowed on: Did the chopped liver need more salt? The kishke was nice and fresh, and well-baked. Speier's. She dished up a with curiously hesitant hand, as though the food or cutlery were alive, or as though the minutest difference in quantity given or withheld was of some particular import. She was sure he would like the chicken giblets soup. It was a very tasty soup. A pity, some of the miniature parogen that went with it were a little burnt. The girl turned the stove up too high. Such a pity. But here was another one that wasn't burnt that he should have. Have! Have! They were very small. Made with very nice chicken fat . . .

After the meal she read him a letter from her son, to whom, last year, for the sake of being in a rounded family, the orphaned grandchild she had been rearing had been sent. It was amusing to see, when she went out, she told him, how many Africans in the street recognised her and greeted her as "Martin's grannie!" After such a long time they still remembered, and asked how Martin was.

When the maid had washed up and left the kitchen with her own meal to eat in the servants' quarters, Auntie Sarah told him about the black woman's troubles. "She has to share a room with two others. It's very unpleasant. No privacy. And one of the others is a drunkard. There was such trouble there the other night. Fighting and screaming. The police came. But they are always so ready to hit and arrest. So cruel. That is the way she has to live. I feel so sorry for her. Her husband has been trying for seven years to get a bus driver's license so that he can improve himself. He got it at last a few months ago and she was overjoyed. But now he has lost his job because they found that he is an alchoholic. Isn't it heartbreaking? And now I'm so worried about her daughter. She is fourteen and she wants to leave school and take a job in a factory. I say she should stay in school at least until she is sixteen and try to become a nurse or a teacher. There is so little for them. If she goes to a factory she'll mix with bad types and become a loafer. Goodness knows what will become of her. It worries me so. But what can they do? They are so poor, so poor!"

And her "they" was general: she was bearing a weight for all the underprivileged in the land. Felix wondered if she would feel any lightening of heart when she made her proposed move to Israel, to be with her son and Martin and the other grandchildren. It was to be, instead of the nearness of these African poor, the oppressions of the khamseen and the obstinate ferocity of Al Fatah. The cares of the world were not escapable, and acknowledging them was a part of Auntie Sarah's respectability. This was different from revealing the broken edges left by the clouts of her personal disasters — and Felix felt himself, during the two or three hours of his visit, to be enclosed in a clean well-padded nest, or washed over by resistless ripples of orderliness (resistless, since even his presence did not disrupt their rhythm).

He was putting on his jacket in preparation for

leaving, and speaking with some animation about a project of his that Auntie Sarah had asked about, when the accident took place. For emphasis he flung out a hand, and over went a vase. It was an elaborate piece of cut-glass and it shattered. In his contrition he reached to pick up one of the pieces and caught the ball of his thumb on a blade-fine edge. Then he stood upright, burning with apologies — but expecting to exchange them with his aunt for reassurances, dismissals of guilt, phrases of comfort.

Instead, she appeared to be stricken by the loss. "Oh dear, oh! The cut-glass. Oh, you should be careful. It was an accident, but, oh dear, oh dear! One of a pair . . ." She looked at its double at the other end of the sideboard, as though it had been damaged by the destruction of the first. "Cut-glass . . . I don't think they make this kind of thing anymore . . ."

It was a minute or two before the accident began to leave her feelings at rest. It had plainly given her a shock that went deeper than it seemed to warrant. She was soon to move, to break up her home. There was one awkward item the less to be transported or disposed of (who, in this generation, would want this style of ornament?). But to her, it must have been a crystal of silenced memory, an heirloom intended for Martin perhaps, an emblem of the fragile continuity that made it matter to be respectable, to go on being respectable, to go on . . .

At last she noticed the blood on his thumb.

He wondered, as, with her composure still not

completely restored, she dressed his thumb, what else in her world would fall to pieces if she were made to know all that was in him. The dark red disorderliness of his life.

Invisible Worm

"I want to give you joy."

The bones of her face were almost naked. Yet the transparency gave not onto the skeleton but onto spirit, making a paradox of her presence among ordinary people, in ordinary lounges and motor-cars, in Johannesburg. Once she had presented herself to Felix, the rest of whatever had been reality was displaced. She was the familiar, unrecognised reality under everything, making all the meaning of his life draw to one sharp focus and filling him with a religion as much as with love.

Dr Peter Williams had spoken to him about Lu-cilla Maxwell, a "tormented" girl whom he and his wife were trying to help, and had shown Felix a drawing from her hand, a portrait of finespun pencil lines that breathed onto the paper more than a face, a life.

The first time Felix met her at the Williamses' house, she spoke little, but with an intensity that involved her body in a considering agitation, as though she hunted through her being for the phrases precise and vibrant enough for her meaning, which she brought out with a prayerful pressing together of her hands. She seemed begging indulgence, apologising for the strength of her feelings, the intelligence of her discriminations.

Felix was talkative, being encouraged by Peter to repeat for the other guests his anecdotes of several recent adventures. But hardly a direct word passed between himself and Lucilla Maxwell. This was the party season and within days he saw Peter again. Lucilla had mentioned to Peter that Felix had been in her thoughts since that evening. Flippant to mask his surprise and pleasure, Felix responded, "Well, I haven't exactly forgotten her, either . . . "

At Peter's New Year party, as before, the room threw up some strange barrier between them for though they communicated with their eyes, they were hardly allowed the opportunity for the exchange of a few words, and none tête-a-tête, during all the hours of the party. Either of them seemed at every moment to be detained in talk with someone else. She had come with two young men from her university who were up in Johannesburg for the vacation. For almost an hour, as the party drew to a close with a lingering handful of guests, one of these escorts held the floor with a strange, sophisticated yet confused harangue against Robert Graves's deification of the female. Felix, concerning himself with logic, was one of those who occasionally offered a counter-argument, qualification or question. Meanwhile Lucilla sat at the opposite side of the room, silent, but intently listening.

At last the party broke up. Peter had promised to drive Felix home, but now Lucilla urged him to accept a lift with her instead. She had a two-door car, and one of her escorts was driving. Felix was given the seat beside the driver. He chattered and gave directions as they wove through the suburbs. He was being anecdotal again, resigned to tempering the otherwise blocked night by this minimal communication with the girl.

She was seated behind the driver, and it was as though she breached a wall when, with no more prelude than a cry — "Oh, Felix!" —, she thrust herself between the heads of her two friends, threw her arms around Felix's neck and, suddenly in the wrench of sobs, laid her head on his shoulder. He was struck into a silence, out of which he could only fetch, once or twice, her name, as he stroked her head. Was it simply sorrow that had so unexpectedly overwhelmed her? He felt that it was something else. The evening had destined a communion between them, and now, in the last minutes, but still the first hours of the new year, it was coming to fruition.

The two young men seemed oblivious to what was happening. Felix gave his last few directions in a chastened voice. When they reached his house, Lucilla left the car and stood while he moved toward his gate. He turned and said to her, "We must see each other."

She pressed her hands urgently together and brought them twice up toward her face and down with emphasis, as she responded: "Soon! Soon!"

Having got her telephone number from Peter, he spoke to her next day. And soon she was with him — at his house, at hers, at the nearby resort lake, at the bird santuary. She told him how long she had known of him and wished to meet him; she wanted to draw his portrait, to read his writings, to show him things she had written, to know and be known to him. There had been turmoil in her life and unsuccessful loves. She had been engaged last year to the scholar who had been discussing his thesis on Graves, but things had gone wrong. She had been briefly, extraordinarily involved with another of Peter Williams's friends, but had felt stifled and distorted by the formal religious demands he had made of her. She leaned on Peter and his wife, who were solicitous, generous, understanding. But (something other than words said it) it was for him, for Felix, that she had been looking, waiting.

The worship of Lucilla was hardly emergent in him yet when he spoke about her once more with Peter, who seemed to be committing her to his care. There was something he felt Felix might be able to do for her. Felix argued his own possible unworthiness. His blocked sexuality had driven him to childishly lurid manoeuvres in the past: he had forced a twisted intimacy out of situations in which girls had turned to him for some kind of support, respite, illumination. Whatever wholesome intentions he might start with, his urgencies might overwhelm him and he might put Lucilla into a difficult, if not hurtful situation. But it seemed that by his ingenuousness he transformed his warning, in Peter's eyes, into a reassurance.

His frankness was pressed from him by an exhausting weight of history. At thirty-seven, all the strung-out years of silly, obstinate desire, and the few punctuating episodes of gratificaiton that soon went sour or were cut short, had, he thought, worked a boyish romanticism out of him, set him to oscillate betwen cynicism about his chances and a hardboiled greed. He was neither optimistic nor clean. An enduring hopefulness had fallen away lately, as his cleanliness had done long ago. So he was small and dry, gravelly against himself and his circumstances when Peter brought Lucilla to him, but it was as if her coming was the very medicine he needed.

The third time they were together at his house, she put into words her gift of herself to him: "I want to give you joy." If he wished he might take her in bodily love now; she would give him this if he required it. But there would be an imperfection. They had a need to grow a little more in their closeness. She was disposed to his desires, but if he could wait . . .

She wanted to give him joy. The words almost were enough. It was a joy to be moving with her toward the ripeness of a belonging together that would be perfect—joyful and spiritual at once. Yes, he would wait. Not, certainly, because Lucilla apart from the wonder of her face, was almost bodiless, emaciated to an emanation of feminine grace draping stark bones. He acquiesced in the postponement because it was in favour of perfection. That was what their embrace would manifest. His sense was, for both of them, of finality and arrival. After long wanderings, confusions, torments (she had slash-scars on her wrists), they had arrived in each other. In him, he felt, in his recognition, she could rest in consummate peace.

They were in a state in which the word "forever" did not need to be spoken. "We'll have a little house," she murmured once day as they lay together, "where you'll write and I'll paint . . . " And her words absorbed the whole of future time. Then, after ten days or so, it came out that there were circumstantial priorities. She had to return almost immediately to her university and attend to certain matters before she could begin the last year of her course in painting. In not having prepared him for this disruption she was, in a manner, diminishing its importance: it concerned no more than time and space. Moreover, she imbued her departure from him now with an aspect of peril for herself — in leaving him she was going from a protective nest naked into a storm of forces that oppressed, abraded and cut at her. He, whom she had found during this vacation, was all in all — but there were matters which must be completed before she was free simply to be with him. She was driving down with one of her two escorts of New Year's night. The other, her ex-fiancé, had left earlier.

The intensity of happiness in the ten days he had had with her lifted Felix beyond commonplace judgments or commonplace facts. More than her electing and centering upon him, more than her beauty (though each of these was an expression of the central thing), it was the way she thought that seemed so spiritual to him.

Yet it was only after she had left that he gave himself up to the religion of Lucilla. In his letters to her he penned its gospel. Her letters to him were rarer, but they consisted of many pages, accumulated piece by piece over weeks, in pencil, ink and typescript, making him party to intimate flashes of emotion and perception. They were gifts of herself which bound him ever more to her, and the gift-like aspect was emphasized in her always sending the thick-packed envelopes by Express so that they arrived at unpredictable times, even, once, on a Sunday morning. They were the prophesies and revelations of the religion — always marvellous in their poetry and in their proof of her continuing bond with him. More than once she telephoned him across the hundreds of miles, to unburden herself of some unease and receive the comfort of his voice. The comfort of his voice!

When she had been explaining why she must go, she had suggested that he might come to visit her. Her letters intimated that she bent desperately under barely definable burdens and demands. Now Felix had the opportunity of a lift to her town and back after three days. He telephoned her and explained the circumstances. "Do you want me to come?"

"Ah, Felix, do you want to come?"

"Of course! You know I do. But what I want to be sure of is, is it right for you? Now?"

"If it's right for *you*, then it's right . . . and you

must come."

"Well, then I'm coming . . . where can I stay?"

"Shall I book a room for you in an hotel? . . . It'll be wonderful to see you."

He loaded himself with gifts: marrons glacés, a favourite volume of prints from his bookshelf . . . And he prepared his heart for more than a renewal of the magic of those ten days at the start of the year: he was coming to her now as her lover.

In the event he was and was not. He entered the quite foreign country of her student life. A welcoming note from her was waiting at his hotel, and soon after his arrival she was there, running to him in the lobby, bare-footed and in flowing white, and giving him a kiss which sanctified his coming.

She had a flat in the house of Mrs Young, one of her lecturers, which she shared with a classmate nicknamed Dozer who was the subject of the first portrait Felix had seen from her hand. Dozer was big-boned, strong, earthy and full of slangy playfulness. When it came to words that moved toward abstractness, she was slow, absorbent, passive. Felix saw quickly that the two women complemented (but Lucilla was complete!) and needed each other. And they were hardly separable. This was one thing that disappointed him. Dozer was easy to be with, responsive to all that was anecdotal and playful in him, while an occasional remark, gesture or anecdote of her own, not to speak of Lucilla's tender respect for her, intimated a richness of resource beneath her unpretentious surface. But for so many hours of his little time her presence was between him and his angel.

All the same, it was clear that she knew of the intensity between them — perhaps she knew more about the intricacies of Lucilla's feelings than he did himself, and she was, in all things it seemed, subservient to Lucilla's wishes. And so there were intervals when Felix was alone with Lucilla. But neither then did simplicity come. Late on his second evening, when their happy leisurely supper was over, Dozer went out. Lucilla let Felix draw her into her room where they lay on her bed feeding intimacy with murmurs and caresses. He became, as every reason, hope and circumstance had been leading him to become, urgent for her body. But she held his hand and gazed with tender sorrow into his face as she said, "No. No. Please, Felix, forgive me. I can't now. It wouldn't be right for me now."

"Why not?"

"Please understand, dearest Felix — please don't be angry. It's because of George . . ." George Wright was the young music lecturer who had accompanied her on her drive from Johannesburg. "George loves me so much. He has wept because I won't go to bed with him. And I'm sore at having hurt him so. I'd be thinking about him. I wouldn't be happy with you. I would feel wrong."

Felix was silent. His clearest thought was, I shouldn't have let you go away — I should have taken you when you offered me joy. He could put up no fight, make no assault on her decision, not even question of her reason for it, not only because the reason expressed her character, but because this refusal, cutting through the nerve of his expectancy, caught up an old pattern of his experience and paralysed him. To have the old rejection of his bodily reality re-enacted by her, was to suffer a small death, a wrenching apart of matter and spirit.

He somehow contained it. The thought that she was in crisis over George Wright, and that the sexual proscription was bound to this, helped him. And moreover, the physical expression was a marginal part of the apocalypse she represented to him. He was willing to suffer for its sake. He had to recognise in her, despite all mere events and obstacles, some profounder completing of himself. He felt it, and she spoke of a matching recognition of inner completeness for herself in him. They had more than sex to live for together.

So he contained the shock. But as one contains an internal hemorrhage. During hours when they were with Dozer and other people, while he was sitting to Lucilla for his portrait in the big communal studio at the university, when he was alone in his hotel room, he was assailed by questions: Why was he here? What had he come for?

In the end it was the portrait that justified his visit. One of Lucilla's torments during the preceding weeks had been a creative block — and painting was a lifeline to being and meaning for her. He watched her at work; she was smeared with paint, backing off constantly from the easel to stare desperately at her work. He felt he was witnessing more than a process, an agony of incarnation which, by paradox, freed the spirit through the very act of its material imprisonment.

After his second day of posing, when the existence of the portrait was assured, they were visited after supper in the flat by Mrs Young, whom Felix had already met more than once. The progress at the studio was unknown to her, since this was the weekend and Lucilla and Dozer had been exercising their privilege, as senior students, of access at any time. Lucilla was sitting beside Felix when Dozer asked playfully, "Should we tell your secret?"

Lucilla responded with a shy nod, but before Dozer could speak, Mrs Young scanned their expressions and said, "I can guess. You're going to be married . . . "

Amid embarrassed laughter, Dozer said, "Oh, no! She's got to painting again . . . A portrait of Felix."

The appropriate congratulations were given and afterwards the faux pas was not referred to, but for Felix the air rang with its reverberations. It demonstrated how outwardly visible was Lucilla's bond with him, and it expressed also the social acceptability of a consummation that might have belonged only to the realm of his fantasies.

Another incident hit even more strongly at his doubts about Lucilla's happiness or peace in his presence. On the last evening of his stay, Dozer, who had made her affection for him very plain, said to him in Lucilla's presence, "Why don't you come and live with us?" Lucilla was silent, but unprotesting, unsurprised. He felt that she and Dozer must have discussed the suggestion before. All the same, perhaps because indeed Lucilla herself had not given the invitation, he could only treat it as a kind of joke, to be countered, at least provisionally, with arguments of its impracticability and his commitment to tasks at home.

But there it was, a gesture made, a value acknowledged, a possibility opened. It salved the sore of his disappointment, so that not many days later he was telling Moh and Dad that he might marry Lucilla. And something in his manner made them receive the news with solemn pleasure and no protest about her being Gentile or the problem of his earning a living. Within two months he visited Lucilla again, making the journey by train. This time there were no shocks, no climaxes of disappointment, but neither were there, until almost the last minutes before his departure, episodes to relieve his pain at her remoteness, his bewilderment over the question of why she had permitted him to come: her manner, whenever intimacy might have been possible, expressed tolerance for his presence, a desire to be good and gentle toward him, but an unreadiness, an incapacity to make their deep bond manifest.

She was painting a large self-portrait, in which the whiteness of her skin was created by the interwrithing of strokes of a range of different colours. From some angles it took on the aspect of a thing most cruelly flayed. From others, when all blended into the fragile oval of the head, it was the face of a child who had walked through Hell. She gave him, had drawn *for* him a pencilled self-portrait that was an unequivocal expression of grief. Why did he not read it as a message to himself? Because she was tender enough to give him the drawing. Because she was his religion. "Let me be your monk," he begged her. Her grief was parcel of her holiness, her martyr's passion. If she would accept him he would have no need of manhood. But this plea of his only disturbed her.

She had painted a mysterious crucifixion. He studied it for hours as he sat in the studio in which she and Dozer worked while a tide of fellow students and friends flowed around them. Toward the end of his stay he wrote down some lines, a dialogue that symbolised his interpretation of the painting.

Hesitantly, he showed it to Dozer, who insisted that Lucilla see it. When she had read it she was breathless with gratitude. "Thank you, thank you! You've shown me the truth of my painting. This was what I was trying to express without really knowing in my head. Please, oh please, may I show it with the painting when I exhibit?"

"It would be an honour," he said. "But are you sure you want to do that?"

"Yes, yes! I must do that."

A few hours later, as they were driving through the rainy evening to the station for his train back to Johannesburg, she began to glow with the full celebratory responsiveness toward him that had been missing. Her pressed hands dipping toward him, she said, "It's a little miracle the way your poem has helped me to understand what I was trying to do in the crucifixion."

"Well, it's hardly a poem . . . "

"Yes, yes! It's a beautiful poem—and it also speaks about us."

"About us? Oh! I didn't think of it that way."

"But it does, it does! The truth came out. It's a confirmation, about you and me."

Just as last time her portrait of him had been the revealed purpose of his visit, so this time it was his poem.

The mid-year vacation brought Lucilla to Johannesburg, with George Wright, who stayed with her at her parents' home. Her complex relationship with him and with her parents, her inability to keep at her painting even though she had a room to use as a studio, each laid its own stress on her feelings. There were Peter Williams and his wife, and there were other friends, old worshippers, would-be suitors. Yet in the absence of Dozer, who was spending the holiday month with her parents on their farm, she was strangely alone and naked in the world. And she turned to Felix, relying on his full acceptance, for some sort of shelter. The month was broken into, broken up, by socializing and chores, by her illnesses, and the daily hours of her efforts to paint. Yet they were frequently, for hours on end, simply alone with each other, when she manifested a need of him, just him, and in this she re-created him as only gods create. This was what had to be, what, for some arcane reason, was being post-

poned, but only postponed. This year of separa-
tion had to be done with: it was involved with art,
which was part of the same spiritual fruition that
included their love. But he was waiting for her
final return to him. It was essential and inevitable.

Peter was a sensitive amateur photographer, and
one afternoon came to Felix's house with Lucilla
and used a spool or two of film in an attempt to fix
for the eye something of her quality and of the
way in which she and Felix conjoined. Felix was
passive in the operation: the world of cameras
and Lucilla's world were different in his mind,
and he responded protectively to her faint un-
easiness over the whole exercise, though he knew
she had many photographs of herself. Yet they
bowed to Peter's artist's authority when, dissatis-
fied with the long-sleeved blouse she was wearing, he had Lucilla take it off and put on a sleeve-
less pullover of Felix's instead. And they bowed
further. After a few studies of Lucilla alone, Peter
had Felix sit with her and began photographing
them as lovers, and Lucilla permitted this commitment to what would be a sort of public record —
for what Peter was reaching toward in the course
of his score or more of shots was not a personal
memento but an artist's crystallization of their
relationship.

This became clearer after the contacts came
and, Lucilla having returned to university, Felix
was invited to choose the pictures he wanted for
enlargement. Peter added his own preferences
as well, and after the prints were delivered it was
with pride of achievement that he showed them to

many friends. They were an achievement. Lucilla, slender, delicate, was an archetype of love, flight and the need for protection. Felix's image expressed his need and fulfilment, his weakness and strength, above all his bliss. A notion about privacy fluttered in his conscience as he let mere acquaintances see the pictures, but he received their comments and compliments with gratification. He framed and hung one of the studies of Lucilla — in which her eyes and mouth spoke as they had cherishingly spoken to him during their best moments together — and stowed the others as treasure. With her letters, when they came, they sustained him through his rite of passage to the year's end.

The July vacation had also given him a deepened impression of Dozer. Lucilla had read him a letter she'd received from her. Its eloquence startled Felix. It was, in fact, a love letter: that was the only explanation for such an outpouring from one to whom words always seemed to come with difficulty.

But if Dozer was partly Lucilla's involuntary creation, Lucilla's life was seen to lie in Dozer's debt after a crisis a few weeks later. A turmoil of apprehension in Lucilla had gathered into a maelstrom that pulled her from the studio, that flat, Dozer's presence, spun her, in her little car, out along the open road toward nothing, in a renewed pursuit of death. Dozer had found another car, chased and overtaken her, and won her back from suicide by the only power she had, her caring, which seemed the only power that could have saved her.

They learnt later that Lucilla's crisis coincided with the moment of the Prime Minister's assassination. The source of the desperation, her premonition of the social wound that would be felt as such even by many of the politician's enemies because he was murdered in Parliament, lifted Lucilla's suicide attempt above simple personal significance. Felix blessed the protective love of Dozer that had saved her. But he absorbed the incident into the canons of proof of her spirituality.

Nearly three decades past his childhood flirtation with Christianity, Felix, to whom till now Christian affirmations like *Murder in the Cathedral* and "The Wreck of 'The Deutschland'" had been bewildering and repellent, found that his love had led him into strange territory. He could understand suddenly how intensity opened the soul to over-arching truth that dwarfed humanistic hopes, health, happiness — how even life was only a phase in the divine progress. He read Kierkegaard, he read *The Varieties of Religious Experience*. He did obeisance to the idea of suffering, not only because Lucilla did the same, but because she, the artist, the child within the archetypal woman, like Jesus whom she painted and pondered on, suffered and by suffering was characterised and shaped — as though by its means alone she could have come into earthly being and could sustain her destiny.

When in one of his letters he asked her (the question remained unanswered), "Am I to think of you in connection with my bodily love?" it did not mean that his earlier plea, "Let me be your monk," had been hollow: by her wish and acceptance, he would have been empowered to fill this role. But he needed to know what forms of expression he must prepare for their love when they came together at that year's end. His energy lay dormant for the direction of his imagination. Lucilla was his saint (in another letter he wrote, "I'm afraid I've become a spiritual snob. I look at the women I know, at women in buses, on the streets, everywhere, and in no face do I see anything that approaches your soul-beauty"). But he needed to know how they were to be together, what he must make of himself for her.

As the months passed without the definitive signal, the passion he was holding in abeyance for her, at rare intervals flickered and flared in the sexual form. Then, in the desiccating climate of his ignorance his urges began to split him apart. Pending the permission to spring toward her, or the command to sublimate, his sexuality began to rear and roar, baffled and directionless. And its noise became the silence of half-forgotten guilt when he wrote to Lucilla, or read her letters.

He had other letters to write and read besides hers. There were old friendships that had flowered or been kept alive in letters. And there was the endlessly trickling correspondence of his literary business. He prided himself on the explicitness and helpfulness of what he wrote to aspirant writers. It was one of these who suddenly held out to him the possibility of another satisfaction. Among the pieces sent for his comments by a young woman in Kimberley was a story containing a description of female masturbation. It was written with no sign of the nonchalance that was characteristic of the new liberations, and nor did Felix read the sentences with nonchalance. He was fevered by the sense of a wild possibility. "Dear Mrs Steen," he wrote to the author, "You may be surprised by the tone of this letter. I have been in a state of excitement since reading your last lot of work. The three poems are much more controlled and substantial than any you have shown me before . . . But it is the story that has particularly stirred me up, and perhaps not for strictly literary reasons . . . Your frankness suggests a person with whom extraordinary things are possible . . . will you let me write to you with a total openness?"

Veronica Steen's reply expressed ". . . a burning curiosity about the *extraordinary* possibilities you speak of . . . I'd like very much to have a really close communication with you."

Encouraged but still hesitant, he wrote warning her. "You may be shocked and repelled by what I have in mind . . . "

"Nothing can shock me . . ." she replied.

He still hesitated. Veronica Steen was marginal to his life. She held out fires of unreality for him to play with. His real self wanted Lucilla, and the year whose end would bring her to him was rounding out. She would come in late November. It was a question of weeks.

Early in November a telephone call from Peter Williams, who had been told by Lucilla's father, brought the news that she had collapsed with a burst appendix and was critically ill. Felix telephoned Dozer. Lucilla had ignored her pains during the time of winding up toward the exams. She had nearly died during the emergency operation and was terribly weak now, but the doctors thought she would be all right. No, there was no point in his coming down — no one except her mother and Dozer was allowed to see her . . .

A week later a post card from Dozer assured him that Lucilla had pulled through. She was very frail but they thought she would be able to take her exams, sitting in a wheel-chair. They didn't know when she would be well enough to come up to Joey's — probably a few weeks later than had been planned. Dozer would be coming up too, early in the new year.

Felix telephoned again to find out if he should come. For the time being, Dozer explained, they could think about nothing except getting Lucilla strong enough for the exams. They would let him know when it was right for him to come.

The year was whirling apart in a confusion of passions. Felix telegraphed flowers to Lucilla in hospital, wrote her a letter full of thanksgiving for her survival, grieved for her and waited for her. At the same time he hovered for weeks over Veronica Steen's latitude. At last he put it to her beyond the reach of any ambiguity: "What I need is an exchange of sexual intimacies — and I don't want to pretend it will be innocent or natural. If you can't reciprocate at least say you'll bear with my outpourings."

In the second week of December Lucilla came. She had been home for four days before telephoning him. She wasn't driving. She agreed to take a bus and meet him at a city tea room. In her enhanced fragility, her new paleness, she was like a thing unborn but exposed. Something agitated and remote in her manner, once she had kissed him in greeting, made his reaching toward her tense and tentative. She had been very near to death.

"Do you still have pain? Are you over it all now?" he asked.

"I'm tired."

"Yes, I understand that. You shouldn't have come out today. You should have let me come to your house, told me which bus stop to get off at . . ."

She shook her head with a firmness born of desperation. "I'm tired of relationships."

When he had taken it in he protested: "But we haven't found our relationship yet!"

She nodded and nodded. "But I'm tired, so tired . . ." She would say nothing better that day.

This wasn't the end of things. As, since their first ten days, he had felt that she had been in his life from its beginning, so, now that she was pronouncing this negation, she was not closing him out of her life, nor herself out of his. She was freeing herself from a particular net of his expectations (she knew how deep but not how undefined his expectations were), and once this had been thrust off, she was free to stay within his reach.

A few days later on the telephone he said to her, "The thing is, there *is* something that binds us together. You are like . . . you are my sister."

"Oh, yes, yes!" Her agreement was urgent. "But

it's something even closer than that . . ."

For a moment he absorbed the words in silence. "Oh, God! Lucilla . . ." he said at last, "when can I come and be with you?"

"Soon, Felix. Dozer's coming up next week, and soon's I can I'll have the Williamses over to dinner so that they can meet her, and I want you to come too."

He left it. He settled for her acknowledgement of that "something even closer". In fact he had no cause to struggle for: nothing he might do could make Lucilla to him what she was not — nor could any accident undo what she was and remained to him after all. Only his own actions and time . . .

On the second of January he wrote to Veronica Steen, "Thank you for accepting me. Now I'll open to you, my woman, my intimate, my secret love, my joy . . ."

Glossary

The Emergency: restrictive emergency of 1960, declared in the aftermath of the Sharpville massacre.

Kennetjie: game played with sticks.

Koppe: little hill.

Mooi perskes: nice peaches.

Pere: pears.

Slegs blankes: whites only.

Sloots: ditch, riverbed.

Splitbek: tattle-tale, squealer.

Tickey: silver coin, equivalent to about 2 1/2 cents. Now obsolete.

Touleier: team leader for a harnessed span of oxen. Often a small boy who walked ahead, guiding the lead ox by a rope.

Twee sjielings n maandjie: two shillings and a basket.

Valencia song: Valencia,/who the hell/told you/a Jew's penis/has no skin?

Veld: open field.